CU00407393

SONS & DAUGHTERS
of
THE LIVING GOD

Seminars
on
Living in the Power
of the Holy Spirit

TEAM HANDBOOK

John Vaughan-Neil

First published in 2001
by New Life Publishing
60 Wickstead Avenue
Luton Beds. LU4 9DP

© John Vaughan-Neil

British Library Cataloguing in Publication Data
A catalogue record for this book is available
from the British Library

All rights reserved. No part of this book may be reproduced,
stored in a retrieval system, or transmitted by any
means - electronic, mechanical, photocopying,
recording or otherwise - without the prior
written permission of the publishers.

ISBN   1 903623 04 9

Cover design and line drawings by Yvonne Bell 02380 773271.
Yvonne spreads the Gospel through her art in many
ways including vestment design and manufacture

Typesetting by New Life Publishing, Luton
Printed and Bound in Great Britain by
Biddles Limited, Guildford, Surrey

To Mary....
who can still hear the Imperial 66....
and to Kate, Lucy, and Polly

May
the Peace of the Father
the Love of the Son
and the Power of the Holy Spirit
be with them and surround them
forever

Acknowledgements

Having been involved over a number of years in giving The Life in the Spirit seminars published (under that title) by The Word of God community in Ann Arbor, Michigan, U.S.A., I wish to acknowledge with deep gratitude their pioneering work in this field, occasional echoes of which are inevitably caught in these pages.

The method adopted for the scripture sharing sessions is based on an elementary approach to sharing in group prayer, for which I am greatly indebted to Fr.Phelim McGowan, S.J.

In writing the article on the Gift of Prophecy, I have drawn in part on Bruce Yocum's excellent book 'Prophecy' published 1976 by Servant Books.

Scripture quotations are taken from the following sources with the consent of the copyright owners:
The Jerusalem Bible, copyright 1966, 1967, 1968 by Darton, Longman and Todd Limited, and Doubleday & Company Limited.
The Knox Bible, copyright 1945, 1949, the Hierarchy of England and Wales
All quotations are taken from the Jerusalem Bible unless otherwise indicated.

Overall, I should also like to record here my deepest gratitude to all those who, over the years, have overlooked my failings, upheld me in prayer, and with such loving encouragement given me the opportunity to grow and serve.

'SONS & DAUGHTERS' SEMINAR MATERIAL

The Team Handbook is published in uniform with
the Participant's Guide issued in two parts:

PART 1 INCLUDES:
An 'Afterword' on **Seminar 1**
The talk outlines for **Seminars 2-5**
An 'Afterword' on Persevering, following **Seminar 4**
Articles in preparation for **Seminars 7 and 8**
Guidelines for praying and sharing scripture
Scripture for prayer covering Weeks 1-4 of the
seminars.

PART 2 INCLUDES:
The talk outlines for **Seminars 6, 9 and 10**
An 'Afterword' on **Seminar 8**
An article on follow-up entitled:
    'Where Do I Go from Here?'
Prayers
Scripture for prayer following Seminar 8
Praying scripture after the seminars
Suggested further reading.

CONTENTS

CONTENTS

CONTENTS

CONTENTS

CONTENTS

FOREWORD

I am delighted to be asked to write the Foreword to this revised "Sons & Daughters" programme. Having been one of the first to use these seminars when they came out in their original format, I can testify to the fruitfulness of this approach among ordinary members of a Catholic parish.

The seminars that John Vaughan-Neil has produced presume no special theological or scriptural knowledge, no deep spirituality, just a heart-desire to get to know God's love in a personal way in one's life.

Step by step the materials provided lead one, through teaching on prayer and scripture, to take hold of the new life in the Spirit that God is offering everyone. At the same time, for those who, having gone through the seminars, want to continue growing, the seminars provide the necessary tools to go on with the journey into the heart of the Father, a journey that will never cease until we reach our resting-place with Him in heaven. There is here, accordingly, in the words of the team handbook, "something for everyone" *(p.5)*

Throughout the seminars, John's own passionate desire to draw people into the "life abundant" that Jesus came to bring us *(John 10:10)*, shines through. Also evident is his understanding of the difficulties and doubts ordinary Catholics often experience in opening up to the life in the Spirit. "Is this stuff really Catholic?" "Where do the sacraments fit in?" etc. For this reason, the introduction of personal testimonies right at the beginning of the seminars is a master-stroke. There is something about seeing other ordinary Catholics like oneself witness to the life-changing effects of encountering the love of God in a deeply personal way, that has the power to overcome initial doubts and reluctance. I am glad it has been retained, and indeed expanded, in the revised programme.

A feature that is a hallmark of these seminars is the very practical way they lead one to surrender to the action of the Holy Spirit in one's life, as well as yielding to the gift of tongues. Simply urging people to "yield, and it will come" can do more harm than good at times, increasing one's sense of doubt and self-condemnation if nothing seems to happen. John Vaughan-Neil has always grasped the importance of taking people step by step through the process. The revised materials show this in an even clearer way.

The new format presents the meat of the original seminars in an even more convenient, practical format. Nothing is left to chance, or guesswork. The tools to organise, present, and conduct the "Sons & Daughters" seminars are here in abundance.

I wholeheartedly endorse this work and wish John and all

those who make use of these materials all the enjoyment and deep satisfaction that I have experienced in putting on these seminars in my own parish ministry.

> *"Oh, come to the water all you who are thirsty;*
> *though you have no money, come!*
> *Buy corn without money, and eat,*
> *and, at no cost, wine and milk.*
> *Why spend money on what is not bread,*
> *your wages on what fails to satisfy?*
> *Listen, listen to me,*
> *and you will have good things to eat*
> *and rich food to enjoy.*
> *Pay attention, come to me;*
> *listen, and your soul will live."*   (Isaiah 55:1-3)

Fr. Bob Poole
Ottawa Canada
November 2000

SECTION A

INTRODUCTION

THE AIM OF THESE SEMINARS
Welcome to these seminars on living in the power of the Holy Spirit!

There is an emptiness in all our hearts that only God can fill and our deepest longing is to be at one with Him. We hunger and thirst for God, because He made us to *know* Him in a deep and loving personal relationship and we yearn to experience in the very depth of our being the touch of His love. So the first aim of these seminars - through a programme of prayer, scripture, talks and discussions - is to allow God to draw us more deeply into that relationship of love.

We also have another fundamental need. Each of us is only too conscious of the struggle and failure we experience in trying to live out our Christian life in our own strength. We need to live in the power of the Holy Spirit, poured out on us by the Father. The second aim of these seminars, therefore, is to open our hearts and experience in a new way the power of the Holy Spirit working within us.

WHAT WILL THIS ENTAIL?
On our part, we will need to respond to Jesus' call to repent and believe, and invite Him to take His true place as the centre of our lives. It will mean asking Him to change us.

4

All of this, however, is done in the grace He will freely pour out upon us. He is taking the initiative throughout these seminars. It is *He* who will open our ears, give new sight to our eyes and touch our hearts.

On His part, He will bring us more truly alive to know Him in a new way and walk with Him in a new life. This new life will be lived in the power of the Holy Spirit working within us and enabling us to serve the Father, not in our own strength, but in His. It is in this relationship of love, and through the release of the Holy Spirit within us, that we more fully experience what Jesus came to give us, *real* life - 'life to the full' - *His* life, which belongs to every son and daughter of the living God.

SOMETHING FOR EVERYONE

For many, this life will be something totally new. For others, these seminars will provide an opportunity to deepen or restore their relationship with God. All of us will be helped to increase our openness to the working of the Holy Spirit. There is something here for everyone.

PROCLAIMING THE GOOD NEWS

We live with the extraordinary paradox of a Christian community in serious need of evangelisation, many of whose hearts have yet to overflow with the joy and peace that only the Lord can bring, and have yet to be touched by the fire of His love. The only fruitful response to this challenge - the most urgent faced by the church today - lies in each of us being faithful to the Lord's calling, and all that we have received. In the power of the Holy Spirit we must witness

5

to Jesus and proclaim His Good News to our brothers and sisters. This is the mission each of us is commissioned and empowered to carry out in our own unique way -looking to Him with confidence in the knowledge that He is with us, and that the Holy Spirit is clearly and powerfully at work renewing the church throughout the whole world.

Over the last thirty years, seminars of this kind have emerged as a powerful means of evangelisation, and establishing and supporting such seminar programmes is one of the most effective ways in which the local Christian community can be built up. This new material, the use of which has been greatly blessed in the small group and parish seminars that I have been privileged to serve, is offered in the hope that it may prove of value to the church on a wider basis. It should be appreciated in this context that while it takes account of some of the special catechetical needs of Catholic participants, those needs are by no means confined to the Catholic tradition and it is readily adaptable to serve groups drawn from different Christian traditions.

-ooOoo-

THE BACKGROUND
to
'SONS & DAUGHTERS'

SEMINARS ATTUNED TO THE NEEDS OF CATHOLICS
In the course of directing seminars in the prayer group I served during the early 1980s, it became progressively clearer that the content, both of the seminar talks and of the Participant's Guide which we had been using up to that time, needed some radical revision. It needed to be attuned more directly to the needs of Catholic participants.   In addition, it became apparent that we should also take a fresh look at the overall programme, and at the format of the individual seminars, to see how they might best be adapted to suit our needs.
Accordingly, in 1985 I began re-writing our seminars 'from scratch' - as a result of which, not only did the overall programme take on an entirely new shape, but quite a number of new features emerged in the content of the seminar talks and the Participant's Guide.

PRINCIPAL NEW FEATURES
Although they will be evident from the details of this Handbook and the Participant's Guide, it may be helpful to highlight here the principal new features of this programme and its material, which include the following:

THE PROGRAMME

10 seminars, with three 'new' seminars providing for a time of witness to participants by way of introduction, the celebration of the Sacrament of Reconciliation, and detailed teaching on how we are gifted in the Holy Spirit and on the gift of tongues.

Duration of only 4 to 5 weeks - including part of a weekend (a far more manageable commitment for most participants)

Weekly scripture sharing sessions.

THE TALKS

A strong emphasis on witness, with an introduction to the meaning and importance of witness - still a rather weak aspect of our Catholic tradition. (Seminars 1 and 9)

A sensitive introduction to what is at the heart of renewal - emphasising that it is *not* some kind of new church organisation; allaying fears regarding charisms; and helping participants to recognise that they share common ground (Seminar 2)

Special emphasis on the personal impact of Jesus' work of redemption, with teaching on the meaning of the new covenant and what it means to lead new covenant lives (Seminar 4)

Emphasis on Jesus' teaching on the gift of the Holy Spirit, and the specific ways in which we can expect the Holy Spirit to work in us (Seminar 5)

A new 'double' seminar - Part 1 on understanding how we are gifted in the Holy Spirit, and Part 2 on the gift of tongues

(Seminar 6)
Special emphasis on the meaning of our call to holiness and **A**
our commission to witness to Jesus (Seminar 10)

THE PARTICIPANT'S GUIDE

A two-part guide - Part 1 covering the programme up to the Saturday in Week 4 (when participants are prayed with for the release of the Holy Spirit) and Part 2 covering the remainder of the programme.

Detailed talk outlines, with copious background scripture references.

A series of three articles in preparation for Seminar 7 (Celebrating the Sacrament of Reconciliation) - including articles on the Sacrament itself, the importance of forgiving others, and on renouncing any involvement with the occult.

An article on preparing for Seminar 8 (Praying for the release of the Holy Spirit)

An article on the gift of tongues.

A 'realistic' programme for praying scripture throughout the seminars, with additional scripture themes for prayer when the seminars are concluded.

Detailed guidelines on praying scripture, keeping a prayer journal, and small group scripture sharing.

TEAM HANDBOOK

A comprehensive guide on presenting the seminars, which assumes no previous experience, and covers among other things:

- the seminar team and its work
- planning and administration checklists
- guidelines for group leaders
- guidelines for witnessing
- guidelines for speakers (orientated to 'first timers')
- additional speakers' notes
- follow-up suggestions, with a re-union celebration programme and detailed guidance for workshops on the gifts of tongues and prophecy
- recommended reading

John Vaughan-Neil

Introduction and Background taken, with revisions, from the first seminars distributed privately in July 1988

-ooOoo-

PREFACE

IMPROVEMENTS

The basic structure and content of the 'Sons & Daughters' programme remains unchanged. However, the opportunity has been taken to make a number of improvements to the text and layout of the original seminars, the most significant being as follows:

OVERALL PRESENTATION

The major improvement is in the presentation of the Participant's Guide. This is now published in two booklets, in place of the original nine leaflets. This is a much more convenient format for participants, which will also greatly assist the administration of parish and other large group seminars.

The material of original Leaflet No. 7 (on Celebrating the Sacrament of Reconciliation), together with the article on 'Involvement with the Occult' (originally a 'hand-out' at Seminar 4), now appears towards the end of Part 1 of the Participant's Guide under the new title: 'Preparing for Seminar 7'.

The material originally at the end of Leaflet No.5 (entitled 'Come Holy Spirit') also now appears towards the end of Part 1 of the Participant's Guide under the new title: 'Preparing for Seminar 8'. Seminar 8 itself has been given a new seminar title: 'Baptised with the Holy Spirit' and an opening 'keynote' scripture from Acts 1.

PSALM REFERENCES
The numbering of the psalms has been altered throughout to follow that of the Hebrew text, *which is the numbering adopted by most modern bible translations (and by the Grail translation of the psalms).*

TALK OUTLINES AND ARTICLES
The article on 'Involvement with the Occult' (to which the speaker refers participants at the end of Seminar 4) has been expanded to avoid its being misread.

The title of Seminar 5 has been changed to 'New Heart - New Spirit', with a new opening 'keynote' scripture from Ezekiel 36.

The examples given in the Seminar 5 talk outline of the specific ways in which the Holy Spirit is manifested have now been extended. (See Part 1 of the Participant's Guide - pages 26-31.)

The talk outline for Seminar 6 part 1 (on being gifted in the Holy Spirit) has been expanded: the first three pages are entirely new. (See Part 2 of the Participant's Guide - pages 1-8.)

I have come to realise over the years that unless participants can be helped to recognise that they are *personally* called to be on the Father's business, then teaching on the gifts of the Holy Spirit may be largely a waste of time. It is only when we accept the job, that we know how badly we need the gifts!   This new material addresses that problem.

It takes about an hour to do justice to the talk as now out-lined, in which provision should be made for a five-minute break about half way through. **A**

In Seminar 6 part 2 (on the Gift of Tongues), paragraph 4 of the original article, entitled 'Opening to this gift', has now been expanded under four new paragraph headings, beginning with: 'How do I yield to the gift of tongues?' (See Part 2 of the Participant's Guide - pages 14-17.)

The outline for Seminar 10 contains a new paragraph, headed: 'Constantly surrender to the power of the Holy Spirit' (see Part 2 of the Participant's Guide - page 35.)

A new article towards the end of Part 2 of the Participant's Guide entitled: 'Where Do I Go from Here?' gives participants some encouragement and hints about what to do once the seminars are over.

PRAYERS

A new section towards the end of Part 2 of the Participant's Guide contains some prayers which participants may find helpful as part of their daily prayer.

SUGGESTED FURTHER READING

The list of books for suggested further reading has been extensively revised.

Although a number of the books listed are, sadly, now out of print (e.g. Cardinal Suenens' classic 'A New Pentecost?'), they are sufficiently important to mention in the hope that some participants may have the opportunity to borrow them or purchase them second-hand.

THE TEAM HANDBOOK

Under Section C ('The Participant's Guide'), new guidance and background is given generally on the revised article 'Involvement with the Occult' (contained in Part 1 of the Participant's Guide), and also with particular reference to the subject of participation in non-Christian religions.

The original commentary on the scripture programme is now contained in a new section (Section D) entitled 'The Scripture Prayer Programme.'

Section F ('Planning the Seminars') contains a new, extensive commentary on two important and related matters, under the titles: 'Who are these seminars *for*?' and 'Getting the numbers 'right" (see pages 38-39).

The original cross-referencing of the Speaker's Notes to the talk outlines was unduly complex and has been omitted. Section K ('Seminar Guidance Notes') now contains detailed (revised) guidance on how to pray with participants for the release of the Holy Spirit, and how to help participants yield to the gift of tongues (see K/8).   It also advocates the distribution of some 'follow-up' material at the end of Seminars 9 and 10 (see K/9 and K/10).

Section L ('Follow-Up to the Seminars') contains a revised programme for a reunion celebration supper and some entirely new material giving detailed guidance for a workshop on prophecy - including how to help participants yield to the gift, and an article which may be used for the talk (see pages 138-151).

A

Section M ('Recommended Reading for Team and Group Leaders') has been extensively revised.

John Vaughan-Neil
Pentecost 2000

SECTION B

THE SEMINAR PROGRAMME

THE OUTLINE

Week No.	Seminar No.	Seminar Theme
1	1	*'Life to the Full'* Introductory talk and information evening with testimonies
	2	*'Come and Drink'* Understanding what is at the heart of renewal
2	3	*'No Greater Love'* God's love for us
Week 3	4	*'Free Indeed'* The work of Jesus, restoring us to the Father and establishing the new covenant
4	5	*'New Heart - New Spirit'* The work of the Holy Spirit, and what the Holy Spirit promises
Sat a.m.	6	*'Power from on High'* Understanding how we are gifted in the Holy Spirit (2 part seminar)
Sat p.m.	7	*'Repent and Believe'* Celebrating the Sacrament of Reconciliation

Week No.	Seminar No.	Seminar Theme
	8	*'Baptised with the Holy Spirit'* Mass of the Holy Spirit with prayer for new life in the Holy Spirit
5	9	*'Only Have Faith'* Continuing your walk in faith: trusting, praying and persevering
	10	*'A New Creation'* Growing in your new life and learning to live in the power of the Holy Spirit

B

GENERAL NOTES

FIVE WEEK PROGRAMME

In order to maintain the general 'pace' of the programme, it is very important to try and keep it to within the 5 weeks shown in the outline. In order to achieve this:

Seminars 2, 3, 4, 5 and 10 will normally take place on the same day (e.g. Thursdays) in Weeks 1 - 5 of the programme.

Seminar 1 will be held two or three days (only) before Seminar 2 (i.e. *both* in Week 1).

Similarly, Seminar 9 will be held two or three days before Seminar 10 (i.e. *both* in the last week).

Seminars 6, 7 and 8 will be held on a Saturday or over a weekend.

SEMINAR 5

There should be a gap of at least one day between Seminar 5 and the weekend Seminars 6, 7 and 8. The participants need a little time to prepare for Seminar 7, and to take stock generally in preparation for Seminar 8.

SATURDAY/WEEKEND SEMINARS

Although participants do need time to absorb what they are receiving, and to open themselves to what the Lord is doing, it has been found in practice that by incorporating part of a weekend the programme can be kept to five weeks (or less), and still make proper allowance for participants' needs in this respect. Indeed, this arrangement brings with it some further distinct advantages. Not only does the weekend allow time for 3 seminars - including the 'double' Seminar 6 - it is also a time when, by comparison with week-day evenings, most participants are more alert and relaxed. They also have the opportunity to share a meal together and generally enjoy each other's company. All of this fosters greater cohesion and mutual support within the whole group at the crucial stage of its preparation for Seminar 8.

If special circumstances prevail so that neither Saturday nor weekend seminars are feasible, the programme can be adapted accordingly. However, in order to maintain its general momentum (*particularly* in the follow-up to Seminar 8), **every effort should be made to avoid its extension beyond 6 weeks.** In this situation, one alternative would be to have Seminars 5 and 7 in Week 4, 6 and 8 in Week 5, and 9 and 10 in Week 6.

SEMINARS 8, 9 AND 10

Ideally, no more than two or three days should elapse between Seminars 8 and 9. Participants need assurance and encouragement following Seminar 8, particularly in the form of the teaching in Seminar 9, as to how they are to move forward. As with Seminars 1 and 2, Seminars 9 and 10 should also be planned to take place, if at all possible, in the same week (i.e. Week 5) of the programme.

B

VENUE

If the group of participants is small, the seminars should if possible be hosted in the home of one of the team members (assuming there is sufficient accommodation to allow for the small group sessions). This is the ideal setting for the seminars because it provides the unique warmth and hospitality that such a home can provide.

If the seminars are being run for a prayer group, the venue for Seminars 1 and 9 should in any event be that of the prayer meeting. In this context, those members of the prayer group who are not participating give their support to those embarking on the seminars at Seminar 1, and join with them in thanksgiving at Seminar 9.

If arrangements can be made for the participants and team to spend the weekend away together - staying overnight on Friday and/or Saturday - so much the better. This arrangement takes maximum advantage of the opportunity presented for relaxation and fellowship as a group.

TWO-HOUR EVENING SEMINARS

With the exception of the weekend Seminars 6, 7 and 8, it

is advisable to allot two hours for each seminar. On first consideration, this may seem a long time. However, it should be borne in mind that the seminar is broken up into a number of activities, and its length is really dictated by the following three factors:

- The whole group needs a reasonable length of time to pray together at the beginning and end of each seminar.

- There is a lot to be covered in each of the talks, and speakers will generally need up to 40 minutes to do any sort of justice to their theme.

- The small group sessions need sufficient time to allow for full participation in a relaxed atmosphere. If group leaders are anxious to push participants along because the timetable is too tight, it will detract greatly from the quality of the sessions.

Allowing two hours for the evening seminars will also enable an 'over-run' of up to 15 minutes to be absorbed without much difficulty, which will happen on occasion, especially where there is a large number of participants. For example, the small group discussion of the talk could be reduced to 20 minutes and the final gathering for prayer could be confined to a short thanksgiving.

A detailed planning checklist, with supplementary notes, is contained in Section F and the suggested programme for each seminar is set out in Section K.

THE PARTICIPANT'S GUIDE

C

TWO-PART GUIDE
The guide is offered as a 'companion' for the participants
during the seminars. It is issued in two parts:

PART 1 INCLUDES:
An 'Afterword' on **Seminar 1***
The talk outlines for **Seminars 2-5**
An 'Afterword' on Persevering, following **Seminar 4**
Articles in preparation for **Seminars 7 and 8***
Guidelines for praying and sharing scripture
Scripture for prayer covering Weeks 1-4
                          of the seminars
*There are no talk outlines for Seminars 1, 7 or 8.

PART 2 INCLUDES:
The talk outlines for **Seminars 6, 9 and 10**
An article on the gift of tongues
An 'Afterword' on **Seminar 8**
An article on follow-up entitled:
      'Where Do I Go from Here?'
Prayers
Scripture for prayer following Seminar 8
Praying scripture after the seminars
Suggested further reading

The division of the Participant's Guide into two parts happens to provide a relatively neat 'before' and 'after' split, with Part 1 leading up to the weekend seminars. Its purpose, however, is to ensure that participants are not distracted, or possibly put off altogether, by the Part 2 material (in particular the article on the gift of tongues) at a time when they are not ready for it.

THE TALK OUTLINES
These are principally for the use of the speakers. It is important to note that they are **not** meant to be studied by participants before each seminar.   Participants may, however, find the outlines helpful if they happen to miss one of the seminar talks or wish to review a seminar theme either during or after the seminar programme.

THE SCRIPTURE PRAYER PROGRAMME
See generally Section D

'AFTERWORDS' ON SEMINARS 1,4 and 8
There are several important 'afterwords' - on Seminars 1, 4 and 8 - which participants should be encouraged to read *soon* after those seminars.

PREPARING FOR SEMINAR 7
There are a number of articles towards the end of Part 1 of the Guide, under the heading 'Preparing for Seminar 7':
  • *The Sacrament of Reconciliation*
  • *Forgive and You Will Be Forgiven*
  • *Involvement with the Occult*

Participants need to be given reasonable time to read through these articles. With this in mind, their attention should be drawn to them *at the end of Seminar 4*, encouraging them to go through them in good time prior to our celebration of the Sacrament of Reconciliation.

C

INVOLVEMENT WITH THE OCCULT

The article under this title is very important, but is necessarily quite brief. A great deal more could be usefully said on the subject, but to do so in the context of the seminars would create an imbalance that could prove to be highly counter-productive.

One could enlarge on so many points in the article: for example, the author would not count Judaism among the 'non-Christian religions' referred to under 'Other openings to the occult'. But if that exception were stated, the article would have to address why it was excepted, with reference to the teaching of Vatican II, and the further questions such an exception raises.

It is as well to be warned that the article on 'Involvement with the Occult' often attracts criticism - usually from participants who have little understanding of spiritual warfare, let alone any experience of deliverance ministry. If voiced, these criticisms need to be answered (or referred to someone in the team who is best able to answer them).

Group leaders should, as far as possible, avoid any discussion on the article in the setting of the small groups. If questions on the occult are raised *prior* to Seminar 4, it may be appropriate to draw the attention of the participant to the fact that this subject will be touched on by the speaker or team leader at the end of Seminar 4.   In some cases further discussion of the subject may best be left until then.

NON-CHRISTIAN RELIGIONS AND OPENINGS TO THE OCCULT

The subject of the danger of participation in non-Christian religions (referred to under the paragraph headed 'Other openings to the occult') is quite complex and is sometimes the subject of very ill informed criticism. It may be important to note, therefore, if the warning concerning non-Christian religions is challenged, that it is supported by a number of very authoritative sources:

• Fr. Michael Simpson S.J. (while a member of the National Service Committee for Catholic Charismatic Renewal in England) published a three part series of articles in Good News in 1988 entitled: 'Our Approach to Non-Christian Religions', in the second of which (Sept./Oct. issue) he wrote as follows: 'In our actual encounter with non-Christian religions it is clear that not all practices are healthy or capable of being integrated within a Christ-centred faith. There is a danger of evil or demonic powers being released when people enter the spiritual realm without being safeguarded by Christ .... The forces of spiritual evil are very powerful and where people have sought spiritual experience or power in an egocentric way and not in obedience and submission to God then they have basically followed the same way as Satan and have laid themselves open to these demonic forces.'

• John Barr - a Pentecostal minister with considerable

experience in deliverance ministry, who served for many years in the docklands of East London - has lectured extensively in the United Kingdom on deliverance ministry, and consistently warned Christians of the danger of demonic oppression arising from contact with non-Christian religions.

C

• The specific reference to spiritual oppression directly linked with Hindu gods and goddesses is taken from an important interview given in 1978 by Fr. Rufus Pereira (who also has extensive experience in the field of deliverance ministry) and published by Francis MacNutt as Appendix 2 to his book 'Deliverance from Evil Spirits' (Hodder & Stoughton 1996).

PREPARING FOR SEMINAR 8
At the end of Seminar 5, participants will be encouraged to read carefully through the article towards the end of Part 1 of the Guide entitled 'Preparing for Seminar 8'. This is intended to help them to take stock at this stage in the programme, and to discern in particular whether they now wish to pray for the release of the Holy Spirit at Seminar 8. *It also explains how group leaders are to assist their group members in this discernment process.* This is a major step, and some participants will really struggle with it, right up to Seminar 8 itself.

DISTRIBUTION
Part 1 of the Participant's Guide is given to participants on registration. Part 2 of the Guide is distributed after Seminar 6.

SECTION D

THE SCRIPTURE PRAYER PROGRAMME

DAILY PROGRAMME, WITH FOLLOW-UP
The Participant's Guide contains a daily programme for praying scripture throughout the seminars, and also provides some additional themes to help participants to continue praying scripture in the weeks immediately following the end of the seminars. *The programme commences THE DAY AFTER SEMINAR 2, with the readings for Day 1 of Week 1.*

INTRODUCTORY GUIDELINES
Part 1 of the Guide also contains clear guidelines on the following:

- How to pray scripture
- Keeping a prayer journal
- Sharing the Word in the small group
  scripture sharing sessions

Participants will need to study these carefully in time to commence the scripture prayer programme after Seminar 2.

SCRIPTURE FOR PRAYING
The programme has been planned with one end in mind: the participants are *praying* this scripture. They are not

'studying' it, let alone just 'reading' it, and selections of short passages have been chosen as most appropriate for this purpose.

This praying of scripture, coupled with the small group scripture sharing sessions, is such an important channel for the Lord to speak to the hearts of everyone participating that *nothing should be allowed to detract from it.*

Accordingly, the scripture prayer programme contains no suggestions for any further 'optional' scripture reading or study. It should be borne in mind in this context that, for many Catholics, reading *any* scripture on their own is still something unusual, and experience shows that simply establishing their regular daily time for praying scripture will itself involve considerable effort for many participants. For the same reason, suggestions for further general reading are relegated to the end of Part 2 of the Participant's Guide.

D

The comments above must not be taken as in any way discouraging the running of a seminar bookstall (on which see 'The bookstall' in Section E). This can provide a service of great assistance to participants during the course of the seminars, without in any way 'threatening' the scripture prayer programme.

RETROSPECTIVE SCRIPTURE PROGRAMME

It is worth noting that, with the exception of Week 4 of the programme, the scripture programme is *retrospective* - based on the theme of the preceding seminar. With this arrangement, the participants come to the scripture in the light of what has already spoken to them in the seminar talk.

Furthermore, they are encouraged to pray through any passages of scripture that may have touched them deeply in the course of the talk, in place of any (or all) of those contained in the following week's formal programme. There is also another practical advantage in this retrospective arrangement, namely that it may avoid sub-conscious feelings on the part of some participants that praying scripture is some kind of 'homework' in preparation for the next talk.

N.B. It is ***essential*** for the team to be thoroughly familiar with the contents of the Participant's Guide (and in particular the Scripture Prayer Programme), and to understand how it all 'works'.

-ooOoo-

SECTION E

THE SEMINAR TEAM
AND ITS WORK

COMPOSITION OF THE TEAM

The seminar team comprises:

The team leader

The group leaders

All those responsible for the following, which form a vital part of the seminar teamwork:

- music
- greeting
- registration
- refreshments & accommodation
- bookstall
- sound and recording
- visual aids

BASIC ROLE OF PRAYER

Seminars are built on prayer - not least that of the team, who should all pray earnestly (and as appropriate with fasting) for everyone participating in the seminars.

Small group leaders have a special responsibility to pray for each of the participants in their group.

If team members can elicit the support of prayer partners, or other groups, in praying for the seminars, so much the better.

KEYNOTE DISPOSITION - EXPECTANT FAITH

The team will be aware that the Lord has drawn them to serve His people, that He is with them in what they are doing, and will work powerfully through them to draw participants to know Him in a new way.   Throughout the seminars, in whatever they are doing, the contribution of each team member should reflect this awareness, and bear the mark of their expectant faith.

THE TEAM LEADER

The task of the team leader is to give effective leadership to the whole team, to have overall pastoral responsibility for the participants, and to be a source of encouragement for everyone.

The leader should be able to give one or more of the seminar talks and to lead the group in praying for the release of the Holy Spirit at Seminar 8.

The person chosen as leader must, therefore, have the maturity to fulfil this role, as well as meeting the same requirements that fit team members for group leadership.

THE GROUP LEADERS

The group leaders' role is to encourage their groups in reaching out to the Lord, building up the participants' faith and supporting and helping them in whatever way they discern best.

Group leaders should look to the Lord to equip them for the task in hand, enabling them to guide the members of their group with wisdom and confidence. They should count on the Holy Spirit to manifest His gifts, in particular giving them wisdom and knowledge to meet the needs of individual participants and His word in prophecy to encourage and guide them.

Great care must be taken in choosing the group leaders. Particular attributes and experience are required for particular jobs, and small group leadership is no exception. This is *not* a job that anyone can do just because they have experienced the release of the Holy Spirit and are committed to serving the Lord. Many such people (including some who *want* to serve in a group leadership capacity) will not be suitable.

E

The basic attributes and experience which all group leaders should have may be summarised as follows:

- They will have been through some form of Life in the Spirit seminars.
- They will have a certain maturity in living in the power of the Holy Spirit.
- They will have the natural ability necessary to lead the small group sessions, and are fully open to the gifts of the Holy Spirit enabling them to recognise and respond to the needs of the participants in their group, and to encourage and guide them.
- They will be outgoing, enthusiastic, and totally committed to the work entrusted to them.
- They will not be experiencing emotional strain or other difficulties that could impede their ability to

serve their group and function well as part of the team.

The more group leaders are drawn from the group or parish for which the seminars are being held, and are therefore known to the participants, the better. It is inevitable, however, that where seminars are arranged for large numbers, the team will often have to be augmented by group leaders invited from other groups or parishes.
Detailed guidelines for group leaders in leading their scripture sharing and discussion sessions are contained in Section H.

MUSIC MINISTRY

Good music ministry for the seminars is very important, since it gives a special dimension and depth to the prayer of the whole group. It will also on its own account help participants to experience a new freedom in prayer, and - with so many songs based on the word of God - minister with great power to their individual needs.
The music ministry should play a predominant role in the prayer time, which opens each seminar, and will also have a very special role during the weekend seminars.
If you are not fortunate enough to have an established, mature music ministry within your group or parish, then it is worth all the effort to locate such a ministry and invite them to join your team for the seminars.

GREETING AND REGISTRATION

The ministry of greeting, and handling registration, is a

special role, which not only gives participants a warm welcome, but can also establish 'one-to-one' relationships that may prove to be significantly helpful for the participants concerned. By reason of their affinity with one of the greeters, some participants may on occasion feel able to share more freely with them than with other members of the team or their small group.

The team would do well to include greeters (where possible) among those responsible for registration.

THE BOOKSTALL

With the wealth of excellent literature that has accompanied the renewal of the church over the last three decades, it is an excellent idea to run a seminar bookstall. Participants are hungry for good spiritual reading. The following points, however, on the operation of the bookstall should be kept in mind.

The team member running the stall should have some familiarity with the books on sale, so they can assist participants who may be looking for particular help. If necessary, they can also refer to another member of the team for guidance.

Care should be taken in the selection of books, in particular to exclude material which could prove too demanding or would be otherwise unsuitable for those embarking on the seminars and in the early stages of living in the power of the Holy Spirit. Books, for example, on special aspects of the occult (e.g. witchcraft) would not be suitable for the seminar bookstall. Your guideline should be: 'If in doubt,

E

leave it out.'

It is a good idea to build up the content of the bookstall as the seminars progress, rather than displaying all books from the outset, giving brief advertisements for some of the new titles as they are added each week.   This maintains a continuing interest in the bookstall.

The bookstall should not be open at times when it would distract participants from the business in hand.

The list of books at the end of Part 2 of the Participant's Guide may provide some help in selecting books for the stall.

REFRESHMENTS AND ACCOMMODATION

As with the greeters and those dealing with registration, the warmth of the welcome given by those chosen to provide refreshments and arrange the accommodation will have a significant impact on participants.

SOUND AND RECORDING

Sound and recording is a crucial service to the seminars. Unless the group is small, speakers ought to have the facility of a good microphone and amplification. (This should also be checked out *in advance* to ensure that it is in working order on the night!)

It is a substantial bonus if arrangements can be made to have the talks recorded and cassettes run off for participants who are interested. This is always well worth the trouble to arrange, since the cassettes can be of considerable help to participants both during and after the seminars, and are often circulated to a much wider audience than those attending.

VISUAL AIDS

To what extent visual aids will be used depends, of course, on the individual speakers. If any speakers do require equipment for visual aids (ohp, screen, flip chart etc.) one of the team members should be responsible for making the arrangements to have the equipment available for the seminar(s) in question. Sadly, the use of visual aids is somewhat neglected in this field, and it is an area where a truly gifted team member, working in close collaboration with one or more of the speakers, could make a significant contribution to the quality of presentation of the seminar talks.

E

TEAM MEETINGS

It is important that the team works as a body. In addition, therefore, to praying for each other, the team should meet together before each seminar. The basic format suggested for the team meeting is as follows:

15 min . . . . Prayer and ministry for the speaker and
team. Prayer for the participants.
(It may also be necessary to 'pray up' the
room/venue with holy water or blessed salt.)

15/20 min . . Report back by group leaders to the team
leader on the last seminar, raising any
difficulties or particular needs that
emerged, and discussing how they should
be met. It is important that all group
leaders and, as appropriate, other team

members, are involved in this process.

5 min . . . . .Reminders on any special points for the
current seminar; any relevant admin.
notices; closing prayer.

It is a good idea for as many of the team as possible to meet
(if only briefly) after each seminar, just to thank the Lord
together and to minister briefly to each other as may be
appropriate. However, it is only to be expected that the
need for group leaders to remain available to participants
after the seminar formally closes may sometimes preclude
the whole team from gathering in this way.

Urgent matters arising at any seminar should, of course, be
brought to the team leader's attention immediately the
seminar closes, rather than be held over to the next team
meeting.

CONFIDENTIALITY

Participants will on occasion ask for help on something
shared in confidence with their group leader or another
member of the team. If that help would best involve
another member, or several members, of the team, the
participant's consent must be obtained before their help is
enlisted. It should be explained to the participant that the
other member(s) of the team would in turn be asked to treat
the matter as confidential.

Participants usually readily understand that the team is
working as a unit, and agree to other members being involved.
However, if for any reason, a participant is unwilling to allow

other members of the team to assist them, then it is crucial that the team member in whom the participant has confided should maintain strict confidentiality in the matter in question - *regardless of the fact that they may thereby be unable to give the participant all the help that they need.*

-ooOoo-

E

SECTION F

PLANNING THE SEMINARS

PRAYER SUPPORT FOR PLANNING
Well in advance of the seminars (and in the case of parish seminars, in full liaison as necessary with the parish priest), the team leader will need to hold several planning meetings to cover the tasks set out in the checklist below. Those responsible for planning will need the prayer support of the team from the outset in working through the planning process and resolving whatever difficulties they encounter.

PLANNING CHECKLIST
The following matters will need to be addressed in planning the seminars:

Who are these Seminars _FOR?_
In many cases it will be perfectly obvious whom you wish to attract to the programme. However, there will be instances where there are quite a number of options. For example, the programme could be offered as part of the parish programme preparing adults for baptism/confirmation and reception into the Church (known in the U.K. as the RCIA); or to certain parish organisations. Again, it could be limited to young people preparing for confirmation, or - as will often be the case - offered to the parish as a whole. It could also be offered to the whole deanery; or it might be organised as

an ecumenical outreach with other local churches. It is important to discern, therefore, at the outset whom you should aim to attract to the programme. Your answer (which will clearly affect many other aspects of your planning) may itself be heavily influenced by your consideration of the next issue concerning *numbers.*

Getting the Numbers 'Right'
Surprising as it may seem, through a mixture of over-enthusiasm and unbounded optimism, teams occasionally fail to give adequate thought to the question of numbers, with serious consequences for the running of the programme. It is vital to take into account the following two points:

F

The number of participants that a team can *properly* cater for is directly dictated by the number of people available to act as group leaders.

The best number for small groups is between 5 and 6 participants for each group leader. (To allow for proper participation in the small group sessions, the *maximum* workable ratio is probably 8 participants per group leader, and even this would require some adjustment to the evening seminar timetable.) [See further on this Section K/2 - Admin Checklist for Seminar 2.]

It would be quite reckless, therefore, (for example) to throw open a seminar programme to the whole deanery, if you anticipate 80 people will attend from your own parish, and an estimated 40 from the other parishes in the deanery, if you have only 10 group leaders available. If your predictions on numbers are right, this will result in your small groups averaging 13 people! Even assuming that all the group leaders could handle groups of this size (which in practice is most unlikely), they could not possibly conduct the scripture sharing and discussion sessions allowing adequate participation by all members within the limits of a two hour evening seminar. The small group sessions would be wrecked!

In determining, therefore, whom the seminars are to be aimed at, it is essential to make a sound estimate of how many group leaders are available to you, and as good an estimate as you can of the number of participants likely to attend. If these estimates show that the number of participants likely to attend would be so high as to require group allocations of 9 or more participants per group leader, then serious consideration has to be given to having an advance booking system, operating on a 'first come, first served' basis.

It is interesting to note in this context that these seminars have been run on many occasions with an invitation extended to adjoining parishes on the basis that they will supply group leaders to serve the number of parishioners they are bringing. This has worked out extremely well. Also, some churches have a long experience of running courses similar to this with an advance booking system - strictly controlling the numbers of participants attending the course in order to ensure it runs properly.

Establishing the Team
This may include inviting, as necessary, additional group leaders/music ministry from outside. [See Section E.]

Fixing Dates for the Programme and Follow-up Sessions
For guidance on the programme dates, see generally Section B. The follow-up dates may not be established at the time of the initial publicity. Nevertheless, it is important for the team to try and fix dates for the sessions as early as possible to ensure that the whole team is available for them. The participants also need reasonable advance notice of the follow-up dates - possibly best announced at Seminar 4, or the weekend seminars (at the latest).

F

Ordering Team Handbooks and the Participant's Guides
Of the team, at least the team leader and all group leaders should have a copy of the Team Handbook- in addition to a copy of the Participant's Guides - *well in advance* of the start of the seminars.

Booking the Venue and Accommodation
On booking accommodation see, in particular, the notes on the programme for Seminars 6,7 & 8 on pages 96-97.

It is difficult to generalise about accommodation, since so much depends on the venue and the numbers participating. Two points, however, are worth noting. First, unless the group is particularly large (i.e. running into hundreds) speaking from a platform does 'distance' the speaker from the group, which is unhelpful. Second, where possible seating for participants should be arranged in a 'horseshoe' fashion, which gives the group a sense of community.

Publicity

This will include drafting announcements, designing posters and handbills, distribution and timing. It might also include speaking at Sunday masses. Great care should be taken over the type and distribution of publicity, which needs to be *limited* to those whom the team is hoping to attract. [See 'Who are these seminars *FOR?*' above.]

When promoting the programme, it is important to describe the theme of Seminar 6 in general terms (as shown in the programme outline in Section B - page 16). Specifying the exact nature of Part 2 of that seminar (on the gift of tongues) could be off-putting for some potential participants.

Inviting Team Members to witness

At least two team members, and ideally three or four, should give their witness at Seminar 1. It is obviously desirable that they should have a mixed age range, and be as varied as possible. *They should all study the Guidelines for Witnessing set out in Section I.*

Almost everyone approached to give their witness will find the prospect quite daunting, and they will genuinely believe that they could not possibly speak for more than five minutes. In fact, when they come to prepare their witness, none of them will find any difficulty in speaking for 10/15 minutes, and in many cases they will find it difficult to confine their witness to the time allotted. Each person should be assured along these lines at the outset.

Choosing and Inviting Speakers

All speakers should have experienced the release of the Holy Spirit. Before inviting outside speakers, the team should pray for guidance as to whether the Lord is calling some of their own number to give one or more of the talks. A natural diffidence in putting oneself forward needs to be watched lest it impair true discernment in this area.

'First time' speakers will need to study Sections A, I and J of the Handbook. If they do not already have it, each speaker should be supplied with a copy of that part of the Participant's Guide which contains the talk outline for their seminar. If they do not have a copy of the Team Handbook, it may also be helpful to let them have a copy of the Introduction to Section K (page 68) and the Speaker's Notes for the relevant seminar.

F

The person invited to introduce the celebration of the Sacrament of Reconciliation should also have a copy of Part 1 of the Guide to which they may wish to refer.

Speakers' Accommodation

Some speakers may need overnight accommodation - with a member of the team, and may need to be met at the railway station.

Inviting Priests for Seminar 7

In inviting priests to be available to celebrate the Sacrament of Reconciliation (and one of them to introduce it), it is advisable to have a contingency arrangement with one or two priests on 'stand-by' to allow for your maximum number of participants. Once registration is complete, the arrangements can then be made firm.

Inviting a Priest to Celebrate Mass at Seminar 8

The celebrant for Mass should be someone who is totally 'at home' with what is taking place, and would be happy (if invited) to join the team in praying with participants for the release of the Holy Spirit.

Music Ministry

This will include arranging a supply of books or ohp equipment and transparencies, and a suitable range of hymns with some balance between those familiar to the group and new material.

Sound, Recording, and Visual Aids
[See Section E.]

The Bookstall

The team member responsible may need help from others in the team in establishing a list of books and estimating the number of copies that ought to be ordered. Some orders may have to be placed well in advance. [See Section E.]

Greeting and Registration

Registration will include preparing registration forms, providing name tags, and collecting registration fees.
There can be very understandable reluctance to charge any registration fee for the seminars and there may well be

circumstances where it is inappropriate to do so. In most cases, however, participants are glad to make a contribution, particularly when it is explained to them that it is purely to cover running costs - including the cost of their own Participant's Guides and offerings to visiting speakers (including their travelling expenses).

Where there is real concern that some participants may be unable to afford the full registration fee, the use of envelopes for *all* donations will avoid causing any embarrassment. An announcement on the following lines could be made in the publicity material:

F

On registration, participants are requested to make a single donation towards the running costs of the seminars (including offerings to speakers and the cost of seminar books): a donation of [£10] is suggested. *Please put your donation in an envelope.* (Anyone unable to afford the full donation is invited to make whatever offering they can)'

If this approach is used, envelopes should be available for participants at registration.
Guidelines on offerings for speakers are published by the NSC.

Creche Facilities
In the case of parish and other large group seminars, consideration should be given to whether creche facilities could be offered to parents of small children, especially (for example) for the Saturday morning sessions of Seminar 6.

This may make all the difference for some participants.

Group Leadership Training

The team leader will need to hold a training session for group leaders who are 'first timers' and any who would like a 'refresher course' - just going over the role of the group leader, and the basics of leading the scripture sharing and talk discussion sessions. *Special* care should be taken in dealing with the scripture sharing session, because its structured approach requires very careful preparation and application on the part of the group leader if it is to be run properly.

It may, in some cases, be a good idea to invite *all* the group leaders to attend this session (i.e. including those who have already worked on the 'Sons & Daughters' programme) - and use it as an opportunity for them all to meet and pray together.

-ooOoo-

SECTION G

REGISTRATION

SMALL GROUP SEMINARS

In cases where seminars are being run for a small prayer group, those who might wish to register should be invited to talk the idea over with a team member who can explain what the seminars are about, and help discern if the seminars would benefit them at the present time.

Careful consideration should be given before extending the invitation outside the group, not merely because in some cases 'outsiders' may not settle in so easily with other members of the group, but the team members may not have the advantage of some prior acquaintance with them.

A similar approach could be adopted for other small groups, possibly holding Seminar 1 as an 'information evening' well in advance of the remaining seminars.

Registration for prayer group and other small group seminars, canvassed as indicated above, should be quite straightforward, and will be completed (save for the odd late registration) prior to Seminar 1.

PARISH AND LARGE GROUP SEMINARS

In more open arrangements, and particularly where large

G

numbers are involved such as parish seminars, personal approach by team members and others may still play an important part in bringing together the seminar group. However, there will still be many participants whose first contact with the course will be at Seminar 1. In these cases, while the bulk of registrations will be completed at Seminar 1, some participants (approximately 15%) may not register until Seminar 2, and probably some further 'late arrivals' will register at Seminar 3.

THE REGISTRATION FORM

The team members in charge of registration should ask participants to complete a simple form, giving the information set out in the sample form opposite.

REGISTRATION FORM

PLEASE USE BLOCK CAPITALS

Name: Mr./Mrs./Ms.
Address:

Daytime phone number:
Evening phone number (if different):

Name of Parish   **G**

Have you attended Life in the Spirit
                    seminars before?   Yes/No

It would greatly help if you would indicate your age group.
Please tick the appropriate group:-

   Under 35   35-50   51-70   Over 70

If creche facilities were made available on the Saturday
[morning] or [morning and afternoon], how many children
would you bring? (Please state whether boys/girls and ages.)

SMALL GROUP ALLOCATIONS

Once the details of those registering are available, the participants can be allocated to small groups. The initial allocation will be made after Seminar 1 and the final one after Seminar 2 (or in some cases after Seminar 3). Generally speaking, registration should be closed at Seminar 3 and no new registrations should be accepted after that seminar. It has to be recognised that after Seminar 3, newcomers would be totally 'out of step' with the scripture prayer programme, and their inclusion would be unsettling for the small groups already established.

The following further points should be kept in mind in deciding the small group allocations:

- Several team members should help decide the allocation to small groups, if necessary liaising with the team leader.
- Generally, the groups should be reasonably balanced with (where possible) an even number of men and women, with a mixed age range. However, single sex groups work very well, as do groups confined to the young age band.
- Unless they are anxious to be together, married couples should be allocated to separate groups. In many cases this enables them to participate more freely than if they were in the same group, and also gives them a wider joint experience.
- Participants who have already done the course (or something similar) are often unaware of the difficulties their sharing can create for participants

who are new to seminars. The best arrangement is to *group them together.* Where exceptions to this recommendation are made, the group leaders will have to be very vigilant in directing the group discussion sessions to minimise the kind of difficulties referred to above.

If the number of participants registering results in the allocation of more than 6 participants in *any* group, the team leader should be notified that the evening seminar timetable will need some adjustment - see Section K/2: Admin Checklist for Seminar 2.

MISSING SOME OF THE SEMINARS

G

The team leader explains at Seminar 1 that the seminars are not just a series of talks, and how important it is for participants to try to attend all of them. It is inevitable, however, that some participants may know in advance that they will be unable to do that, and will usually share this problem either with those handling the registrations or with another team member. If they do so, and it appears that they are certain to miss more than one of Seminars 3-5, then in normal circumstances it is sensible to invite them to consider registering at the next seminar programme when they can do justice to it. It can be explained to participants in this situation that it may be much better to wait than to find that they feel out of step with everyone else, and are uneasy or unable to participate in Seminar 8, when we pray for new life in the Holy Spirit.

Notwithstanding what is said above, it is unwise to make any hard and fast rule on this subject, and there may be circumstances in which a participant rightly decides to join in the programme regardless of not being able to attend several of the early seminars.

Missing the weekend seminars (particularly Seminar 8), or missing Seminar 9 or 10, is also a difficulty for some participants. However, although this is a great pity for those concerned, it should not deter them from registering. Seminar 6 could be made up later using the Guide (or better still a cassette of the morning talks), and participants missing Seminar 8 can be prayed with for the release of the Holy Spirit after Seminar 9 or 10.

PEOPLE WITH 'PROBLEMS'

Everybody has problems, but for most participants their problems will not stand in the way of their being able to participate well in the seminars and benefit from them. There are some people, however, who are under acute stress or whose psychological problems are so serious that - as things stand - they would not be able to benefit from the seminars. The team must be open with such people, and explain to them that the seminars are not right for them at the present time, and give them what help they can - possibly referring them for counselling. There may be others who, though not falling into the category just mentioned, would nevertheless be better waiting a while before embarking on seminars, and they should be advised and helped accordingly.

It is rare to find a participant exhibiting behaviour that is disruptive or otherwise materially impedes others in their participation in the seminars. However, in such a case, the team leader or group leader (possibly with someone in the group who is close to the person) should talk with them, explaining the difficulty for the group, and asking them to withdraw from the programme.

-ooOoo-

G

SECTION H

GUIDELINES for GROUP LEADERS

INTRODUCTION
The small group sessions provide an experience of Christian fellowship at a level that will be new for many participants. As a group leader you should foster this by encouraging your participants to pray for the other members of the group during the seminars, and by generally helping the group to integrate in a friendly and relaxed atmosphere. Through these sessions - sharing the Word together and sharing their response to the talks - participants will receive much of the help and support they need in responding to what God is doing in these seminars.

TALK DISCUSSION SESSIONS

PREPARATION
It is essential that, quite apart from listening carefully to the talk, you prepare for each discussion session by familiarising yourself with the detail of the talk outline (and particularly the scripture) contained in the Participant's Guide and the Speaker's notes for the relevant seminar in Section K.

INTRODUCING THE PARTICIPANTS

After each of the seminar talks, the participants move into their groups for discussion. At the first discussion session (which follows the talk at Seminar 2), before embarking on the discussion, invite everyone to introduce themselves and say a few words as to what led them to sign up for the seminars. This will then lead naturally into a discussion of the talk.

KEY POINTS IN LEADING THE DISCUSSION

Encourage participants to share **one or two points (only)** that spoke to them most deeply during the talk.

The purpose of the session is **not** to ensure that participants fully understand or accept everything the speaker has said, but **to enable the group to consolidate and absorb some of the most important points made by the speaker.**

If the leader identifies some misunderstanding on the part of a participant, they should take the opportunity, *briefly*, to redress it.   However, if a participant raises some *serious* difficulty arising from the talk, then the leader should offer to have a word privately with them about it later. Do not allow the group to be materially 'side-tracked' from the main purpose of the discussion.

Keep the discussion on the right track to meet its purpose. In particular, you should not allow participants to develop any discussion or debate on matters of controversy or criticism (e.g. of the Church's teaching, the participant's parish, a local priest etc.). This is totally counter-productive for the participants, who are there to be built up and encouraged. As with any digressions, it is your job to lead

H

everyone back, gently and *quickly*, to the main discussion.

You may well have someone in your group who is rather effusive and in danger of dominating the discussion. **Don't let them** - whenever necessary, you will have to intervene: "That's another interesting point, John, but let's hold it there for the moment while we hear someone else share. Margaret, is there anything you would like to share on the talk?" Be gentle, but firm.

It is important to try and involve the shy members of the group in this discussion, and if you address them with real interest they will usually warm to it and be glad to participate. Above all, let them know that their contribution is valued by an appropriate word of thanks during the session itself, or later.

Gentleness should mark every aspect of your leading. Be careful not to dominate the discussion yourself, or come over as someone with all the answers. **Listen with the utmost care to what participants are saying.**

If in the course of the discussion you illustrate a point with reference to your own journey in faith, keep in mind the points made in Section I ('Guidelines for Witnessing'). It is very important that any such sharing is pitched to suit your group, so they are not unnecessarily challenged or threatened by what you say.

SCRIPTURE SHARING SESSIONS

GROUP LEADER'S INTRODUCTION
At the beginning of seminars 3, 4, 5 and 10 there is the small

group scripture sharing session, in which the groups share on the scripture they have been praying during the preceding week. *This is a totally different kind of sharing from the discussion sessions that follow the talks* (which is why it is important to hold them at separate times during the evening).

Guidelines on how to share scripture are contained in Part 1 of the Guide. Although participants should, therefore, be generally aware of what these sessions entail, you will need to explain at the start of the first session (i.e. at the beginning of Seminar 3) exactly how the sharing will run, basing your explanation on the following 'model'.

'MODEL' INTRODUCTION

"Those of us who feel able to do so are now going to have an opportunity to share very briefly on some scripture that has spoken to us during this last week. It is a wonderful thing to share the way the Lord has spoken to us in His word, because the Lord builds us all up through His word and we are fed in a special way through this kind of sharing."

H

"Should you feel unable to share, simply tell me (or shake your head if you prefer) when I get round to you. You mustn't worry about that, or think you're not playing your part in the session. Just relax and participate by listening and praying. You may find that you are able to share in later sessions as the seminars progress."

"I shall begin the sharing myself, but before I do so I just want briefly to summarise the basic structure of our sharing, which is explained in the article 'Sharing the Word' on pages 66/67 of your Guide, as follows:

You will read out from your prayer journal just a verse or two that has spoken to you in a special way this last week. The rest of us don't try to follow it in our bibles - we just listen carefully to you speaking out the Lord's word.
You then say, very briefly (I mean 15 -30 seconds at the most!) why it was special to you - how you felt the Lord speaking to you in it.
Last of all, and even more briefly, you tell us the gist of how you responded in prayer. Most important, I mean only the gist of it: **you mustn't read out the prayer response written in your journal.'** (Note: there is an illustration of this is on page 66 of the Guide, which you might wish to read out to the group at this point.)

"After your sharing, we all continue to remain in silence for about a minute, during which time we allow the Holy Spirit to lead us to pray in the quiet of our own hearts in response to what we have heard in the sharing. If the sharing has not struck a chord with you in any way, then simply be still in the presence of the Lord. We then move on the next person's sharing."

"The *whole* sharing shouldn't take more than one and half minutes overall, **during which time the rest of us remain absolutely silent."**

LEADING THE SCRIPTURE SHARING

When you have given the introduction, pray briefly, drawing the group to focus on Jesus, and then start by giving your own sharing following the basic structure.

After your own sharing (and the minute of quiet prayer following it), don't let the sharing move round the group at random: turn to the participant next to you and invite them to share ("George, have you some scripture you can share with us?"). If the participant declines, they should be reassured instantly with a gesture and/or a word ("That's O.K."or "That's fine."). After each person has shared and the group has prayed in silence, do make sure you thank them with a simple 'Thank you', and then move on to invite the next person to share, and so on round the group.

Do not attempt to cajole anybody into sharing, either during the session itself, or outside it. Let participants come to it as the Lord may lead them. Sharing in this way involves a breaking open of oneself, a sharing of what is a most intimate part of one's life. It is an act of great love, and it costs everyone who does it.

H

It is **absolutely vital** that participants follow the direction not to read out their prayer responses from their journals. If any participant begins to do this, you must intervene *immediately,* and explain that the journal is strictly between them and God alone: all they are now invited to share with the group is the gist of their response.

To allow participants - let alone encourage them - to share what they have written in their prayer journals (other, of course, than the verse or two of scripture they have copied out) is to court certain disaster. Not only will they be tempted to 'compose' their prayer response for sharing in the group, but the prospect of their doing so will in turn disrupt their private prayer time - turning the journal into a distraction and a burden, and destroying its whole purpose. It would also damage the confidence of those who have difficulty in keeping a journal or in sharing.

Sharing of this kind is something very deep and intimate. It is not something to be commented on, agreed with or otherwise analysed by anyone, with remarks such as "That's interesting." "That's just how it struck me." "That's beautiful." "I wouldn't have thought God was saying that." *Everyone's sharing should be received in total silence: all comment is out of place.* The group needs to be kept *strictly* to this rule, and it is surprising how - at first - some participants find it difficult to resist making comment. If this happens *you must intervene and restore silence.*

MISSING SOME OF THE SEMINARS

If any of your participants find *unexpectedly* that they are unable to attend some of the seminars, you will need to consider with them whether it may be better for them to withdraw from the programme (with the intention of registering at the next one). In this context, the comments made under this same heading in Section G may be pertinent (see pages 51-52).

-ooOoo-

SECTION I

GUIDELINES FOR WITNESSING

PRAYER

At the risk of stating the obvious, do pray earnestly before preparing the basic outline of your sharing, and when filling in the detail of it. You will not be able to tell the *whole* of your story, so you need His guidance to discern what are the particular elements of your experience that are most appropriate to include in your witness. The Holy Spirit wants to use your 'mini-gospel' to touch the hearts of your listeners: it is vital, therefore, that you remain open to Him throughout the preparation and delivery of your testimony.

WHAT TO SHARE

Your sharing should cover:

a) how you came to experience a personal relationship with the Lord and the release of the Holy Spirit in your life; and

b) how you have changed as a result of that experience.

As to a), this will be a sharing of some of the detail of your own personal search for God and how He drew you to repentance and a new turning to Him.

As to b), in sharing how you have changed, detail some of the major changes which resulted from your experience of a personal relationship with Jesus and the release of the Holy Spirit. These changes may include (among other things) your experience of:

I

61

- just knowing Him, and the peace and joy of His presence within you
- opening to the power of His love working in your life, bringing reconciliation and healing, and changing your relationships within the family and at work
- a new power of prayer in your life
- a new power to resist temptation
- greater depth of participation in the Mass and the Sacrament of Reconciliation
- scripture coming alive for you in a new way
- knowing His guidance in your day-to-day living
- the gifts of the Holy Spirit at work in you as you have reached out in the service of others
- the ability to share more freely with others about His love and forgiveness.

It is how you have **changed** since you have come into a deeper relationship with the Lord and experienced the release of the Holy Spirit (much more than particular 'experiences') that will speak deeply to participants, and enable them to realise that the seminars have something special to offer.

HOW TO SHARE

Tell your story on a personal basis, simply and naturally. You may find it helpful to share your testimony with a member of the team (either directly, writing it down, or by putting it on tape) and get their reactions and comments on it. This will help you to revise any aspects you may have felt unsure about and generally get the balance right. The following summarises a number of things to avoid in your witnessing:

- If you had one, don't go into details about your chequered past! It is quite enough to make general reference to a lifestyle or relationships that were at odds with the way Jesus wants us to live. Details are not only unnecessary, but may embarrass, shock, or distract participants from the main thrust of your witness.
- Try to avoid speaking of 'baptism in the Holy Spirit'. This can be very confusing for some participants, most (if not all) of whom will have received the Sacrament of Baptism. Instead, speak of experiencing the 'release of the Holy Spirit'.
- Also avoid jargon that can distance your listeners. Instead of saying: "God 'laid it on my heart' that-" you can just as easily - and far more effectively - say "I felt God was urging me to-" Your listeners are not likely to switch off if you say: "It was as if God were speaking in my heart" - whereas they might do so if you say: "On Monday morning, God said to me -" The key to cutting out unhelpful jargon is to remember that you are sharing with people who, for the most part, will only rarely (if at all) have experienced God working in the same ways as you have, and they are not familiar with stories of the kind you are telling.
- This first meeting is not the time (if indeed there would be any right time within the context of the seminars) to share struggles you may have had in opening to the giftedness of the Holy Spirit working in your life, particularly in relation - for example - to the gift of tongues. Participants will be asked at the

I

next seminar to lay aside their fears or concerns on the subject of charisms, which will be dealt with fully in their rightful place when we come to teach on our being gifted in the Holy Spirit. They certainly don't want their concerns (if they have any) heightened by hearing your own early misconceptions or difficulties in this area.

- You may have experienced resting in the Holy Spirit. (This is often referred to as 'being slain in the Spirit - a phrase which, with its violent undertones, does less than justice to the gentleness of the Holy Spirit and ought on that account to be avoided.) Although this will undoubtedly have been a great blessing to you, it is nevertheless an experience which few, if any, of your listeners would be able to appreciate. For some your mentioning it could be unsettling. So, unless for some special reason its omission is going to somehow weaken or distort your witness, it would be best to avoid any reference to your resting in the Holy Spirit.

'I'M NERVOUS'

Everybody feels nervous about giving their witness - and not only the first time they give it. Remember, however, that this has a very good side to it, namely, that you will be relying heavily on the Lord to carry you through and anoint what you are saying, which is how His power is released in you. Once you have actually started, you will find that the Lord will give you an inner assurance and peace in 'telling what He has done for you' that will support you throughout your testimony.

SECTION J

GUIDELINES FOR SPEAKERS

*Note: The following guidelines are for
those who are not experienced speakers:*

RELY ON THE POWER OF GOD

Pray throughout the planning of your talk, raising up its
whole content to the Lord so that you may be truly inspired
in the detail of what you say.

Ask the Lord to use you to touch the hearts of the seminar
group.

Do not over-value natural ability as a speaker (although we
should be glad to put at His service what talents we may have
in that direction) or be over-concerned at how inadequate
for the task you may feel. Remember that if the Lord is
leading you to speak, He will be lending His own power and
authority to what you say.

Try not to over-plan your talk. Leave room for the Holy
Spirit to further inspire you in the course of its actual
delivery.

J

KEEP IT SIMPLE: KEEP IT 'REAL'

Keep your talk as simple, down-to-earth, and direct as
possible. At its heart, the message of the Kingdom is
extremely simple, and everybody should be able to follow
what you are saying without difficulty.

USING THE TALK OUTLINES
The talk outlines contained in the Participant's Guide are put forward as a framework on which to build, as you are led by the Holy Spirit. It is obviously desirable that the talk you give covers most of the key points in the outline, and takes some account of the special emphases in the Speaker's notes given for the particular seminar in Section K.

Exactly how you cover the key points, however, and establish those emphases, is entirely a matter for you. To the extent that you are 'at home' with the finer details of the outline, then use it: *but it is vital that you make it your own.* That means in particular taking the opportunity to build into your talk, as appropriate, your own witness (on which see Section I), and illustrating what you are saying by tying it into your own practical, concrete experience of everyday life.

USING SCRIPTURE
Sharing the Word is a key factor in all the seminar talks, so you should carefully pray through your choice of scripture. In addition to supporting what you are saying, the scripture chosen should be the Word that speaks deeply to you personally. In turn, that Word will then be specially anointed on your lips because it will be spoken with the resonance of your own heart's response to it.

DELIVERING YOUR TALK
In order to maintain the flow of your talk, ensure that your scripture references are properly 'flagged' in your bible ('Post It' slips can be very useful here.) Please note that it

will have been explained to participants that they should not try to follow scripture references in their own bibles during the talk itself - unless you specifically invite them to follow a particular text very closely.

Try to keep within the time allocated for your talk: materially overrunning the allocation may risk diminishing the talk's overall impact, and may put pressure on the remainder of the programme for your seminar.

SHARING TALKS

Sharing a seminar talk between two speakers may bring even greater variety and richness to its content and delivery - in particular extending the scope of experience with which participants may identify. It looks, however, deceptively simple. In practice, if it is to achieve its goal, it requires a high level of harmony and general 'rapport' between the speakers. It also requires considerable preparation of the material so as to preclude overlapping (which in turn can sometimes dampen spontaneous departure from the 'agreed' talk). However, if the aim can be achieved, it is well worth all the effort involved.

J

-ooOoo-

SECTION K

SEMINAR GUIDANCE NOTES

INTRODUCTION

This section contains for each of the seminars, (as may be appropriate):

Suggested programme

Guidance notes for:
- the speaker
- the team leader
- the group leaders
- other team members

Articles on:
- witnessing
- how to pray with participants for the release of the Holy Spirit
- how to help participants yield to the gift of tongues
- a general administration checklist

Notes for the speakers are intended to give a little more of the 'background' to some of the key points in the talk outlines, including some which deserve special emphasis because they have been blurred or neglected in the catechesis of many participants.

NOTES FOR SEMINAR 1

"LIFE TO THE FULL"

PROGRAMME

15 min . . . . Welcome by the team leader
Prayer

5 min . . . . Team leader's introduction to witnessing

45 min . . . . 3 or 4 testimonies - each speaker
introducing themselves

10/15 . . . . Summing up by the team leader outlining what
min the seminars are about *(see further on p. 73)*
Introduction of the team
Invitation to all present to enjoy some
refreshments, talk over their reactions to what
they have heard, and - those who wish - to **K1**
register.

35 min . . . . Refreshments/informal discussion/Registration

5 min . . . . Closing prayer
Notices

SPEAKERS

One of the elements in seminars which is so powerful in helping people to turn to the Lord in a new way is the personal witness of the speakers and the team. This witness gives the participants new hope that the Lord can work real change in their lives, and therefore enables them to look to Him with expectant faith.

So what better way to start the seminars than for participants to hear your unique testimony as to how the Lord has acted in your lives, and brought you to new life! Through this witnessing, the Holy Spirit will touch the hearts of the participants, awakening them to the reality of what the Father offers and promises to all who believe in His Son.

Read the team leader's introduction to witness given below, which will help you to appreciate that what you are doing is in the mainstream of the Church's tradition, and follow the Guidelines for Witnessing contained in Section I.

TEAM LEADER

Many of the participants may never have heard anyone give a personal testimony before, and the whole idea of witness may seem somewhat alien to them. It is important, therefore, that before the first speaker, you give a short introduction to what witnessing is about, which will help put participants in a more receptive attitude. The following outline may be useful for you to draw upon.

INTRODUCTION TO WITNESS

Witness is such a weak point in our Catholic tradition to-day - so weak in fact that, for most of us, the very word 'witness' smacks of something entirely outside our experience, something that our Baptist or Evangelical brothers and sisters may engage in, but not us! Which only shows just how impoverished we are in this particular respect - at least for the present. Thank God that He is beginning to bring about the necessary change in us.

The irony is that none of us might *be* who we are to-day, but for the most powerful witness of our contemporaries and our forbears: the word 'martyr' comes from the Greek word 'martus' meaning 'witness'. But martyrs, whether twentieth century or from another era, are not the only example of witnessing within our tradition to which we can look for encouragement and inspiration. For there is another magnificent illustration to be found in the Prayer of the Church, which centres on the inspired prayer of the psalms. Even a casual 'dip' into the psalms reveals that they are positively *bursting* with witness, encouraging and embodying the proclamation of what God has done for all His people:

> 'Alleluia!
> Give thanks to Yahweh, call his name aloud
> proclaim his deeds to the peoples!
> Sing to him, play to him,
> tell over all his marvels!
> Glory in his holy name.
> Let the hearts that seek Yahweh rejoice!'
>
> *Psalm 105:1-3*

K1

71

'When Yahweh brought Sion's captives home
at first it seemed like a dream;
then our mouths filled with laughter
and our lips with song'

Psalm 126:1-2

'With mighty hand and outstretched arm,
His love is everlasting!
He split the Sea of Reeds,
His love is everlasting!
Let Israel through the middle,
His love is everlasting!
Drowned Pharaoh and his army,
His love is everlasting!'

Psalm 136:12-15

and *personal* tribute to God for all His saving help:

'my joy lies in being close to God.
I have taken shelter in the Lord,
continually to proclaim what you have done.'

Psalm 73:28

'I was pressed, pressed, about to fall,
but Yahweh came to my help;
Yahweh is my strength and my song,
He has been my saviour.'

Psalm 118:13-14

'Come and listen all you who fear God,
while I tell you what he has done for me.'
Psalm 66:16

Praying the psalms is one of the Church's deepest traditions, and they show that to witness to the power and love of God working in our lives is second nature to God's people. Remember, it is the Holy Spirit who inspired the psalms, who brought forth their witness from the lips of His people. It is the same Holy Spirit who calls and empowers each of us to witness to God in all our living, and in our own time to proclaim our own personal and unique gospel. Every one of us has our own gospel to tell.

SUMMING UP

Following the testimonies, your summing up should *briefly* cover the following:
- The general aim of the seminars (which can draw on the introduction in Section A)
- The overall shape of the seminar programme (lasting between 4 and 5 weeks, and including 6 more weekday evening meetings, plus part of a weekend in which Seminars 6, 7 and 8 take place)
- The standard evening programme (following that used **K1** for Seminar 3)
- The 'basic ingredients' of the seminars.

THE STANDARD EVENING PROGRAMME

In dealing with this item, explain (in addition to outlining the standard programme) that all those who register will be divided into small groups for scripture sharing and discussion of the talks. (There is no need, however, to elaborate here on how the small group sessions will run - that will all be made clear by the group leaders in due course.)

THE 'BASIC INGREDIENTS' OF THE SEMINARS

In relation to this item, explain that over the next few weeks we shall be praying, following a scripture prayer programme and hearing the Lord speak to us through His word, and listening to a series of nine talks and discussing them. At Seminar 8, those who wish to (only those who wish to) will pray for new life in the Holy Spirit, inviting Jesus to be the centre of their lives, and asking to be renewed in the power of the Holy Spirit.

It should be stressed that the seminars are not just a series of talks, but a supportive framework in which participants are helped to open their hearts to God in a new way. Each seminar builds on the last, so it is very important to make every effort to attend all of them. Inevitably, there will be occasions when some participants are simply unable to avoid missing a particular seminar and in that event they can in part make that up by going through the talk outline privately.

INVITATION TO REGISTER

Emphasise that those who wish to register can do so before the close of the evening. However, anyone who is undecided should come along to Seminar 2 which explains some aspects of the seminars in greater depth. There will be no pressure put on them, and the talk may help them in their decision.

Announce that all those registering need to have a bible and should ensure they pick up Part 1 of the Participant's Guide on registration *and read the guidelines for praying and sharing scripture at the **end** of the Guide introducing the Scripture Prayer Programme.*

CLOSING PRAYER AND NOTICES

Close the evening with a *short* prayer, remind everyone of the date of Seminar 2, and remind the team to hand in their badges at the registration desk.

REGISTRATION

You have charge of the distribution of Part 1 of the Participant's Guide to everyone who registers for the seminars. (With large numbers, it may be better to *give* the Part 1 booklets to participants, rather than simply let them help themselves.) It is, of course, important that you have sufficient copies for all those registering, and for this purpose it is wise for your estimate of numbers to be a little on the generous side.

It is also an excellent idea to give each participant a small notebook to use as their private prayer journal for the seminars. At negligible cost (which can be covered in any event by the registration fee), this emphasises the importance of keeping a journal, saves participants the trouble of obtaining one for themselves, and encourages them to keep it from Day 1.

K1

Your initial allocation of participants to small groups will follow the close of this seminar.[See generally Section G.]

Once group allocations have been done, name badges can be prepared in readiness for Seminar 2.

One of the registration team will have responsibility for preparing name badges for the team and participants. Please note the following:

- It is helpful for participants if a team member's badge bears some colour or marking that identifies them as one of the team.
- The badges for group leaders and participants should also identify the group to which they have been allocated - *showing the group number.*
- All badges should be handed in at the registration desk at the end of each seminar - otherwise team members and participants will be prone to mislay their badges in between seminars, or simply forget to bring them.

In large seminars it is a good idea to identify the assembly point for each group with numbers posted on the wall. These can now be prepared in readiness for Seminar 2.

BOOKSTALL

Ensure you have some bibles for sale at this seminar. In addition, some members of the team may be happy to give you a small stock of bibles to *lend* to participants until they have bought one.

ADMIN CHECKLIST

In addition to Part 1 of the Participant's Guide required for distribution at this seminar, you may wish to provide participants with small notebooks for their private prayer journals (see further under 'Registration' on page 75).
Name badges are to be distributed to all members of the team at the start of this seminar.
Donation envelopes may be required at this seminar. [See Section F 'Greeting and Registration' - page 44.]
It is much easier for your administration if you have a stock of Greeting/'Thank You' cards and give your offering to the speaker on the night/day of their talk.

-ooOoo-

K1

SECTION K/2

NOTES FOR SEMINAR 2

"COME AND DRINK"

PROGRAMME

15 min . . . . Welcome by the team leader
            Prayer

45 min . . . .Introduction of the speaker
            Talk

5/10   . . . . Further 'ad hoc' allocations to
            small groups, if necessary

20/25   . . . .Small group discussion on the talk

20 min . . . .Team leader's introduction to the
            programme for praying scripture

10 min . . . . Closing prayer
            Notices

[Further registrations to be completed
at the *end* of the seminar]

SPEAKER

RENEWAL IS A MOVEMENT OF THE HOLY SPIRIT

This first point is very important for Catholics, who are singularly adept at labelling all kinds of Christian spirituality/outreach as belonging to a particular group. It is extremely important, therefore, that participants understand at the very outset that renewal is not some kind of new organisation or human initiative within the Church, but the movement of the Holy Spirit Himself, renewing His Church. (Cardinal Suenens frequently emphasised this point in speaking of renewal - no doubt because he was acutely conscious of the tendency above mentioned.)

It is also worth noting here that Part 1 of Fr. Peter Hocken's book 'One Lord, One Spirit, One Body' (published in 1987 by The Paternoster Press, but now sadly out of print) ' entitled What is this Renewal in the Holy Spirit?' - makes this same point quite forcibly. It is a masterly introduction to renewal and the best by far that the author has come across.

ACKNOWLEDGING AND LAYING ASIDE OUR FEARS   K2

It is reassuring for participants to know that those responsible for the seminars recognise that participants do have fears, and are sensitive to them. The fears mentioned in the outline are some of the most common: we don't brush them aside, but encourage participants to put them in the Lord's hands, trusting Him to take care of them. In particular, it is important to address the fear that some participants may have of the charisms, asking them to lay aside whatever fears they may have, on the basis that there is much more basic business to attend to for the early part of the seminars. The whole subject of being gifted in the Holy Spirit will be addressed at Seminar 6.

EXPERIENCES THAT UNITE US
It is helpful for participants to recognise that most of them do share some basic, deep experiences in their relationship with God - a realisation that will begin to establish a common bond between them at the very beginning of the seminars.

TEAM LEADER

The evening timetable may need adjustment: see the last two notes under Admin Checklist.
Before the main talk, explain to the participants that as every talk draws heavily on scripture, it is not practical for the speaker to wait for participants to find the reference and follow it in their own bibles. Accordingly, during the talks themselves - *unless expressly invited to do so by the speaker* - the participants should just listen to the scripture quoted.
Again, before the main talk, announce to newcomers, and anyone who has not yet registered for the course, that they should go to the registration desk immediately after the talk, where they will be allocated to small groups on an 'ad hoc' basis to take part in the discussion of the talk. If they wish to register for the programme, they should do so *at the*

end of the evening.
After the small group discussion session, you will be intro-ducing the programme for praying scripture. The Scripture Prayer Programme at the end of Part 1 of the Participant's Guide contains guidelines on how to pray scripture, keeping a prayer journal and sharing the Word, and you should impress on participants the importance of reading these guidelines carefully. It is extremely helpful, however, if you give the participants a quick resume of the points covered in the Introduction (on pages 58-69 of the Guide), *and emphasise that the programme starts with the readings for Day 1 of Week 1 - **tomorrow!***
Also, tell participants how helpful it is to keep a prayer journal, encouraging them to read the article 'Keeping a Prayer Journal' (on page 65 of their Guide), and to start their journals as soon as they have bought their small notebook (or *tomorrow*, if they are being given a notebook at registration).
Announce in your closing notices that registrations for the seminars will close at Seminar 3, and remind all participants and team members to leave their badges at the registration desk for 'safe keeping'.

GROUP LEADERS   K2

This is your first discussion session with your group of participants: be sure you are well prepared for it by carefully studying the guidelines under Section H and doing your preliminary reading.
If, because of numbers, your small group sessions have been

extended to 30/35 minutes, *extra* care will need to be taken to control the talk discussion session to give everyone the chance to contribute. (An extended scripture sharing session should present less of a problem.)

REGISTRATION

Name badges are to be distributed at this seminar - see Admin Checklist below.

Newcomers at this seminar (and others who have not yet registered for the course) are to be allocated to small groups on an 'ad hoc' basis *immediately following the talk,* leaving the completion of registration forms to the end of the evening.

For the purposes of estimating how many copies of Part 1 of the Guide need to be available, in the case of a large seminar usually 15-20% of the number registered at Seminar 1 will be registering at Seminar 2.

Once those newly registered at this seminar have been allocated to small groups, their name badges can be prepared for Seminar 3. (There may possibly be some changes in group allocation for participants *already registered,* who will therefore require badges showing their new group number.) Registrations close at Seminar 3, and the team leader will announce this in the final notices at the end of the evening.

ADMIN CHECKLIST

Name badges, arranged on a table *in alphabetical order* (not according to groups) should be ready for the team and registered participants to collect on their arrival for this seminar.

Part 1 of the Participant's Guide (and prayer journal notebooks?) need to be available for distribution at this seminar (see further under 'Registration' on page 82).

Group number posters may need to be posted up at the start of this and the remaining seminars (see further under 'Registration' on page 75).

Donation envelopes may be required.

If the number of participants registering results in the allocation of more than six participants for *any* group, then **the time allowed for the small group sessions should be extended to 30/35 minutes per session.** To allow for this change, it will be most important to start the seminars *promptly,* and it may be necessary to limit the closing prayer time to a brief prayer by the team leader.

If the timetable needs to be adjusted:

- Resist the temptation to combine the two small group sessions. Experience has shown that for most groups this seriously impairs the scripture sharing session.
- Ask all participants to make a special effort to keep their *talk discussion* contributions brief, so that *everyone* can have a chance to share, and the seminar can end on time.

K2

-ooOoo-

83

SECTION K/3

NOTES for SEMINAR 3

"NO GREATER LOVE"

PROGRAMME

15 min . . . . Welcome by the team leader
. . . . Prayer
25 min*. . . . Small groups - scripture sharing session
45 min* . . . .Introduction of the speaker
Talk
25 min* . . . .Small groups - talk discussion session
10 min . . . .Prayer
Notices

*This time allows a few minutes 'travelling time'
for moving into small groups, and re-convening
for the talk/closing prayer.

SPEAKER

PRACTICAL ENCOURAGEMENT
The subject of this seminar is so vast that it may seem to be

harder than any other talk in the programme. You will see, however, that the whole thrust of the outline is rooted in a practical encouragement to all participants (wherever they stand at present) to turn afresh to the Lord with an open heart to receive His love.

Reinforcing this encouragement by using part of this talk to witness, sharing your own journey in faith, would tie in very well with Seminar 1, and be particularly helpful to any newcomers who may have missed the witness at that first seminar.

UNDERSTANDING WITH OUR HEARTS

This seminar emphasises a key process that develops throughout the seminars. It involves surrendering to God the inadequacy of our understanding of Him, acknowledging our hardness of heart - our stance of self-sufficiency - and asking Him to renew our minds and our hearts so that we can really hear, and understand, and respond to Him. In effect we are saying: 'Lord, I need to enter more fully into the reality of who you are, and all that you have done for me. Open my heart, so I may know you in a new way. Help me to hear and respond to your word of love in my heart.'

LOVE IS A GIFT   K3

One of the widespread misconceptions most crippling to our spiritual development is the idea that somehow I must win or earn God's love. It is as though Jesus' statement: 'If you love me, you will keep my commandments' has been translated in our hearts to read: 'If you keep my commandments, I will love you.' As a consequence, we feel that to win His love we must obey; to retain His love, we must not fail - which is the very antithesis of Jesus' attitude towards us.

With the realisation that God's love is **gift**, freely and unconditionally lavished on us all, many participants will begin to be freed from a struggle they have endured for years - a struggle they know they could never win.

THE MESSAGE IS "I LOVE YOU"

Jesus' submission to death is a great mystery, which like all mysteries is something into which the Holy Spirit enables us to enter more and more deeply as we come closer to God Seeing Jesus on the cross, taking on Himself all our sinfulness, we are naturally led to say: "I played my part in that: that is the fruit of all men's sin, including mine." There is a great danger, however, that for many this response has become distorted in their hearts, and extended to an accusation put into the mouth of Jesus: 'This is what you have done to me!' That is the message we might expect and understand, because it is the kind of message we might have spoken in His place. But it is *not* the message of Jesus spoken on the cross. He Himself declared that He had not come to judge or to condemn, and that on the cross He would draw all men to Himself. We need to come to the foot of the cross and hear the words that are *really* on the lips of Jesus "I love you!"

TEAM LEADER

If there are any newcomers, or others who have not

registered, attending this seminar, you will need to make the same announcement on 'ad hoc' allocation to small groups and registration as you made at Seminar 2.

Check whether your timetable for small group sessions needs to be adjusted (see the last two notes under 'Admin Checklist' for Seminar 2, on page 83).

Since time does not permit you to give the kind of resume you gave at Seminar 2, explain to all those registering at this seminar that they will need to read carefully through the Guidelines for Praying and Sharing Scripture given at the beginning of the Scripture Prayer Programme (starting on page 58 of their Guide). Also advise them not to try and catch up on Week 1 of the scripture prayer programme, but **start immediately (tomorrow) with Day 1 of Week 2.**

At the end of this seminar announce that registrations formally close this evening, and remind everyone to hand in their name badges to the registration desk at the end of the evening.

REGISTRATION

Newcomers and others who have not registered are to be dealt with in the same way as at Seminar 2.

K3

Following this seminar, you will be able to make your final small group allocations. In doing so, it is of course preferable (if you have enough group leaders to go round) to form entirely new small groups, rather than enlarge existing ones, which by now are settling in.

ADMIN CHECKLIST

Badges are to be available at the start, and collected at the end, in the usual way.

In a large seminar there are bound to be some 'late' registrations at this seminar for which participants' books (and donation envelopes?) need to be available.

Now that registration is complete, calculate how many priests will need to be available for the Sacrament of Reconciliation at Seminar 7, firm up the arrangements for those required, and cancel the remainder. In making this calculation, you can expect that about 90% of the participants will avail themselves of the opportunity to celebrate the Sacrament, and - on a *very* rough estimate - they will on average take about six minutes each. It is usual to allow between 1 to 2 hours for celebrating the Sacrament of Reconciliation during the Saturday afternoon programme.

-ooOoo-

SECTION K/4

NOTES FOR SEMINAR 4

"FREE INDEED"

PROGRAMME

The programme for this seminar will be the same as for Seminar 3 (see page 84) - save for the short additional item on 'Involvement with the Occult' addressed by the speaker or team leader after the small group discussion on the talk.

SPEAKER

NEW UNDERSTANDING

Looking again at the work of Jesus, (and the same applies to what we shall look at next week in relation to the work of the Holy Spirit), is not going over old ground just to reassure ourselves that we've always understood it! It is a matter of each of us asking the Holy Spirit to give us a new, deep, vibrant appreciation of what redemption means for us *personally.*

While the universality of redemption (the fact that Jesus died for all men, and won the forgiveness of the sin of all mankind) is something that seems to be easily grasped, we can have great difficulty in coming anywhere near an

K4

appreciation that redemption is highly personal. Jesus did not come simply to save mankind, or to 'save souls': He came to save men and women - to save *me*, to save *you.*

RESTORATION TO THE KINGDOM OF LIGHT

There is a danger that we think of this restoration in a somewhat vague, idealistic way - and are not fully attuned to the reality that the freedom Jesus gives us is something quite radical and concrete. I am intended to experience this freedom personally in my day-to-day living, enabling me to live (in His power) in the kingdom of the Son. We are blessed with the Sacrament of Reconciliation, of which we will always be in need. But we also need to take more fully to heart the words of Jesus: 'Whoever believes in me, *need not stay in the dark anymore'* and the whole thrust of what the first letter of St.John says about sin. Restoration to the kingdom means that *sin is meant to be abnormal behaviour for the Christian - no longer 'par for the course'.*

NEW COVENANT LIVING

In the Mass we drink the chalice of the new covenant. That covenant is down-to-earth, practical and personal. Under the new covenant, Pentecost crowns the work that Jesus did on earth - the Holy Spirit equipping each of us to live out that covenant. It is vital, therefore, to link the events of Good Friday and Easter Sunday with Pentecost. I can live the new life Jesus won for me, because the Father has sent me the Holy Spirit.

TEAM LEADER

There are two matters to be addressed when the participants re-convene following their discussion of the talk. First, draw their attention to the need to read through the articles towards the end of Part 1 of their Guide under the title: 'Preparing for Seminar 7'. The second concerns one of those articles entitled: 'Involvement with the Occult'.

The popularity of dabbling in the occult has seen alarming growth in recent years. Equally alarming, however, is the fact that many people brought up as Christians (and Catholics are no exception here) are unaware that such activities, *however flippant or transitory in nature,* are against the commandments and are spiritually dangerous. One of their consequences can be that we are impeded from opening to the power of the Holy Spirit. It is important, therefore, that participants are acquainted with this reality, and invited to discuss any such involvement, *in confidence,* with their group leader (or another member of the team) in order to receive what help they may need to renounce such involvement.

This subject needs to be raised in a way that does not give **K4** it undue prominence - which could distract participants and/or disturb small group sessions. The most appropriate timing is for you (or the speaker - if you think they will handle this material well) to address the subject at the end of this seminar, after the small group discussion session. You need only speak for a few minutes on the lines of the article, and encourage the participants to read it for themselves and act on it as necessary.

GROUP LEADERS

Be sensitive in the scripture sharing session to the fact that some of your group may be flagging a little in their efforts to pray scripture. This is only to be expected, and they should be gently encouraged not to give up.

Draw the group's attention to the 'Afterword on Persevering' which appears on pages 24/25 of their Guide - which they should read soon after this seminar.

The team leader will be briefly addressing the subject of the occult at the very end of this seminar. If a member of your group discloses to you that they have had some involvement with the occult, it is important that a member (or members) of the team experienced in this area helps the person to renounce that involvement. However, you must first obtain the participant's agreement to approaching others. [See note on confidentiality under Section E - page 36.]

Before any discussion with participants on this subject of the occult, it will be essential that you yourself have read through the article on 'Involvement with the Occult' together with the comments on it under Section C - page 23.

ADMIN CHECKLIST

The dates for the follow-up programme need to be announced at Seminar 5 or after Seminar 6

SECTION K/5

NOTES FOR SEMINAR 5

"NEW HEART - NEW SPIRIT"

PROGRAMME

The programme for this seminar will be the same as for Seminar 3 (see page 84), save for the short additional item on preparing for Seminar 8, to be addressed by the team leader after the small group discussion on the talk.

SPEAKER

THE CHANGE WITHIN

Jesus emphasises that the transition to new covenant living takes place within us, and the Holy Spirit is given to us to bring about this change. In addition to the most striking statement that He will make His home in us, He also gives us the stunning analogy of the water of life, which He gives us, turning into a *spring* inside us. That is the perfect analogy of how the Holy Spirit works within us.

CONCRETE CHANGES - NOT VAGUE ASPIRATIONS

It is important that participants understand that we are not vaguely hoping to become 'better' people. We need to spell

K5

out in concrete terms what they can expect in due course by way of change in themselves, if they now turn to the Lord in repentance, and invite Him to be at the very centre of their living.

TEAM LEADER

At the close of the seminar, after the small group discussion session, give a *brief* synopsis of what is said in the article 'Preparing for Seminar 8' (on pages 52-55 of the Participant's Guide), asking the participants to ensure they read through it carefully before the next seminar, and to pray over their decision.

Remind the team that - *before* Saturday - all those who will be praying with participants at Seminar 8 need to read over the detail of how that will be done (as set out in Section K/8 - pages 109-111 or, for a small group seminar, page 112).

Announce the follow-up programme dates (if fixed).

ADMIN CHECKLIST

Put in hand the preparation of copies (A4 size) of the Prayer for New Life in the Holy Spirit (printed on page 56 of Part 1 of the Guide) for all participants, the team, the speaker and the celebrant at Seminar 8.

Check with the celebrant for Mass at Seminar 8 if he would like any particular readings from the Mass of the Holy Spirit, and also whether he intends to bring any vestments.

-ooOoo-

SECTION K/6

NOTES FOR SEMINAR 6

"POWER FROM ON HIGH"

PROGRAMME

Seminars 6, 7 and 8 are most commonly held on a Saturday, for which a typical programme would be as follows:

9.45 . . . . Welcome by the team leader
              Prayer
10.15 . . . . Introduction of the speaker
              Talk (Seminar 6, Part 1)
              _____
10.45 . . . . ***Buzz group break***
              _____
10.50 . . . . Continuation of Talk
11.20 . . . . Small group discussion on the talk
              with refreshments
11.50 . . . . Talk (Seminar 6, Part 2)   **K6**
              _____
12.50 . . . . ***Buffet lunch***
              _____

[Participants may wish to discuss Part 2
of the talk informally over lunch]

13.45 .... Introduction
14.00 .... Celebration of the Sacrament
of Reconciliation (until 15.30)

——————————

15.00 .... **Tea**

——————————

15.30 .... Team meeting (15 minutes)
15.45 .... Preparation for Mass
16.00 .... Mass of the Holy Spirit - followed by
16.45 .... Prayer for New Life in the Holy Spirit
17.30 .... Close

There are obvious advantages in being able to spread these three seminars over Saturday and Sunday (with Mass on Sunday morning followed by lunch). The participants are free mid-afternoon on Saturday, and they have more 'breathing space' after Seminar 7 and the talk with their group leader. However, it is generally quite difficult to arrange the seminars in this way, and the Saturday (only) arrangement usually works out very well, without in any way 'overloading' participants.

It is very important in planning your programme for the day to give a generous time for praying for the release of the Holy Spirit. You have to ensure that this prayer time is not rushed in any way, still less interrupted by another group who have booked the venue for an event immediately following your seminar. This means that, to be on the safe side, it would be sensible to book the venue until 18.30 - giving a full hour's 'buffer' to protect this prayer time. Depending on how many participants re-gather with the team to pray to yield to the gift of tongues, the day may in any event end closer to 18.15-18.30.

SPEAKER

SOLID FRAMEWORK
Participants were urged at the beginning of the seminars (in Seminar 2) to put aside whatever fears or concerns they might have over the whole subject of charisms, on the basis that this would be dealt with at the right time. Now is the time, and nothing less than this two-part seminar is adequate to give participants a clear, solid framework on the subject.

BEING GIFTED IN THE SPIRIT
Teaching on how we are gifted in the Holy Spirit is quite crucial to participants' becoming open to the various manifestations of the Holy Spirit working within them. Once they understand that we have received the Holy Spirit *in all His giftedness*, and that the gifts are *His* - never ours - working within us, then they will feel free to open to the Holy Spirit in all fullness within them, allowing Him complete liberty to move in them in power, to complete the work of Christ on earth.

K6

The lengthy quotation from Cardinal Suenens' 'A New Pentecost?' given in the talk outline for this Seminar (in Part 2 of the Guide) is justified, and should be used in your talk. Not only does it establish the basic point above mentioned (often thereby correcting a great deal of misunderstanding and poor teaching on the point), but goes on to make another vital point, namely that the Holy Spirit may choose to work in us *in any number of gifts, either successively or all at once, according to the work we are called to do.* The insights given in this part of Cardinal Suenens' book (at pp 82/83) are essential to a true grasp of Chapter 12 of St.Paul's first letter to the Corinthians.

LINKING GIFTS TO SERVICE

The talk outline goes on to emphasise the link between gifts and service. Far from being an occasional spectacular display of 'extras' on the periphery of Christian life, the whole giftedness of the Holy Spirit is essential to the job which the Father has given us to do. We simply cannot live out Jesus' commandment of love and fulfil our commission to witness to the world in our own strength, but only in the power and giftedness of the Holy Spirit. Participants must be helped to see quite clearly that all gifts are 'tools for the job', and directly linked to the service of the community.

THE GIFT OF TONGUES

The teaching given in the article in Part 2 of the Guide should be used as the basis for the talk on the gift of tongues. It should be said at the outset here that this talk is best given by someone who, by reason of their maturity in the use of this gift, can cover the various aspects of its use with conviction arising from their own experience.

Personal experience of allowing this gift to flourish, and prayerful reflection on scripture, points unequivocally to the gift of tongues being an important gift *available to all believers*. The plain fact is that it is the Lord's gift of prayer to His followers: could anything be more fundamental than that?! It is also a key gift that facilitates our opening to so many other gifts that the Holy Spirit wishes to manifest in us.

Given the importance of this gift, and the difficulty which participants might otherwise experience in yielding to it, it is only right to devote a full seminar talk in teaching about it in the run up to Seminar 8.

'HOWLERS' TO AVOID

In teaching on the gift of tongues there are two 'howlers' to be avoided at all costs which are regrettably still in common circulation:

Please avoid referring to it as 'the least of the gifts' which, bearing in mind its importance, is quite an unhelpful description (as well as a plain misapplication of Paul's exhortation in 1 Cor.12 v 31).

Please also avoid telling participants that in yielding to this gift they have to be prepared to 'look foolish for Christ.' Again, this gives a totally wrong impression of this wonderful gift, and can only impede participants' openness to it. In yielding to the gift of tongues, our focus is centred entirely on the Lord - without room for any concern as to what others might think of us.

K6

YIELDING TO THE GIFT OF TONGUES

It is a good idea, after dealing with the question of how to yield to the gift of tongues, to mention that those who wish will have an opportunity later in the day to be prayed with, all together, by the team to yield to this gift.

Do make sure, however, that you emphasise that praying to yield to this gift is **not the main agenda of the day:** the climax of the day (and indeed the seminar programme) is our Mass followed by prayer for the release of the Holy Spirit.

TEAM LEADER

TEAM MEETING

The whole team (as far as possible) should gather for the team meeting at the beginning of this day, praying especially for the Lord's protection for everyone attending, and (unless the venue happens to be a church) sprinkling the room(s) with holy water or blessed salt.

If any of the group leaders have not yet yielded to the gift of tongues, encourage them to take the opportunity at some time during the day (following Seminar 6) to have some of the team pray with them, helping them to yield to this gift. This will enable them to minister more effectively to participants during the remainder of the seminar programme.   (The same applies, of course, to any other member of the team.)

ANNOUNCEMENTS BEFORE THE LUNCH BREAK

Invite participants to have a brief word with their group leader sometime during the afternoon regarding their reflection on 'Preparing for Seminar 8'.

Also invite all participants to come and collect Part 2 of their

Participant's Guide *before* they have lunch. (Do not leave its distribution until after Seminar 7 or 8 because inevitably some participants may need to leave over lunchtime or during the course of the afternoon.)

Draw the participants' attention to the fact that (in addition to the talk outline for the first talk this morning) there is a full article in Part 2 on the gift of tongues, on which the talk has been based.

Encourage all those who will be attending Seminar 8 to read the short 'Afterword on Seminar 8' in Part 2 later this evening or some time tomorrow, and (if they can find time) the talk outline for Seminar 9.

Announce, or remind participants of, the dates fixed for the follow-up programme.

ADMIN CHECKLIST

The team meeting at the start of this day should be early enough to give time to 'pray up' the room/venue (as necessary) with holy water or blessed salt - before participants can be expected to arrive.

A4 copies of the Prayer for New Life in the Holy Spirit need to be available this afternoon for distribution at Seminar 8.

K6

-ooOoo-

SECTION K/7

NOTES FOR SEMINAR 7

"REPENT AND BELIEVE"

PROGRAMME

The programme for this seminar is included in the sample programme given for Seminars 6, 7 and 8 on pages 95-96.

SPEAKER

This is not a formal talk on the Sacrament of Reconciliation, but just a few words by way of introduction (10-15 minutes maximum) *to encourage participants to take the opportunity of celebrating the Sacrament* - particularly if it is a long time since they did so, or if they have found it difficult in the past.

The participants have been encouraged to read the articles under the section 'Preparing for Seminar 7' in Part 1 of their Guide and you may wish to make reference to them in your introduction.

ADMIN CHECKLIST

If there are quite a number of participants wishing to

celebrate the Sacrament of Reconciliation (and most of them will), it is a good idea to free participants from the need to physically queue by having a list outside the confessional for each priest. Participants can then put down their names, deleting them when they have seen the priest. This arrangement also ensures that participants have more free time in which to see their group leader.

Appropriate arrangements should be made to have refreshments available for the *priests* (particularly the priest who will be celebrating mass) during the course of the afternoon.

-ooOoo-

K7

SECTION K/8

NOTES FOR SEMINAR 8

"BAPTISED WITH THE HOLY SPIRIT"

PROGRAMME

See generally pages 95-96

WHEN TO PRAY FOR THE RELEASE OF THE HOLY SPIRIT

Assuming Mass is being celebrated, perhaps the best arrangement is for participants to pray for the release of the Holy Spirit *after Mass has ended.* There are two practical considerations behind this recommendation:

If the prayer time takes place during Mass, and is quite extended (as will certainly be the case with a large group), some participants may not have time to stay for the rest of the Mass.

If some participants rest in the Spirit while being prayed with (or there is some demonic manifestation), some participants may be upset because this is taking place during the celebration of Mass itself.

GROUP LEADERS

During the course of the afternoon you will be inviting each of your group to share with you on the decision they have reached as discussed in the article 'Preparing for Seminar 8'. Refresh your memory of the contents of this article, and pray before you talk with your group members. (Have a copy of Part 1 of the Guide with you for anyone has not yet had the opportunity to read through it.)

It is quite uncommon for participants to decide *not* to pray for new life in the Holy Spirit at Seminar 8. However, if one of your group has decided they are not ready, or seems to have difficulty in discerning what the right course is for them, gently encourage them to talk about it with you, if they can.

Participants should not mistake a measure of nervousness as an indication that they are not ready. Everyone is slightly nervous about the unknown, and the truth is we are never 'ready' for God. What He wants to give us is far beyond all our hopes and expectations (Ephesians 3:20-21).

K8

Above all, however, listen carefully to what your participants have to say, and pray with thanksgiving with each of them, asking the Lord for whatever guidance they need and the courage to follow it.

TEAM LEADER, GROUP LEADERS
AND OTHER TEAM MEMBERS

HOW TO PRAY FOR THE RELEASE OF THE HOLY SPIRIT

Guidance on ways to pray with participants for the release of the Holy Spirit, both in large and small seminar groups, is given later in this section (see pages 109-112).

HELPING PARTICIPANTS YIELD TO THE GIFT OF TONGUES

Guidance on helping participants yield to the gift of tongues is given at the end of this section (see pages 113-117).

TEAM MEETING

The mid-afternoon team meeting will cover (among other things):

- The arrangements for praying with participants for the release of the Holy Spirit - in particular deciding the pairing of those who will be praying with participants. As a general rule it is preferable for participants to be prayed with by the group leaders - the team leader, other team members, the celebrant and speaker(s) helping out where that is considered necessary or appropriate. It is *not* a good idea to invite help from people other than those mentioned above. The participants have established a rapport with their group leaders and the team, and it is with them that they are going to feel most comfortable

during this prayer time.
- The arrangements for any deliverance ministry should the need arise, and queries which anyone has concerning praying with participants generally.
- Prayer for protection for the team, speaker, celebrant and all the participants.

THE TEAM LEADER'S INTRODUCTION

The team leader should introduce the time of prayer for the release of the Holy Spirit by giving a brief outline of the general arrangement, and in addition covering the following points:

- This is not a 'general' prayer time in which to pray for other special concerns (e.g. prayer for healing, problems at work etc.), important though they are. There will be further opportunity for more general prayer ministry after Seminars 9 and 10.
- There will be a short 10 minute break (possibly with some refreshments available) after this prayer time, and all those who wish to pray to yield to the gift of tongues are invited to gather with the team after the break (preferably in the same room used for praying for the release of the Holy Spirit) for a further short time of prayer (approximately 20/30 minutes - depending on the size of the group).

K8

- The essential aim of the seminars reaches its climax with the celebration of Mass and our prayer for new life in the Holy Spirit, and no-one should feel obliged in any way to join in the prayer session after the break.

ADVANTAGE OF THE BREAK

While some participants may yield to tongues while being prayed with for the release of the Holy Spirit, they will usually be very much in the minority. This 'split', whereby participants re-gather after a short break, can be very helpful to the participants in two respects:

Some participants are quite frightened at the prospect of praying in tongues. It helps participants generally, therefore, to be absolutely reassured that praying for the release of the Holy Spirit *is* the essential aim of this seminar; and

The break provides the perfect opportunity for those who wish to do so, to make their way home. No-one is made to feel pressured into praying to yield to the gift of tongues. Precisely because of this lack of pressure, most of the participants do, in practice, return to pray after the break.

MUSIC MINISTRY

There should be some very quiet 'background' music ministry while participants are being prayed with for the release of the Holy Spirit. If the prayer time is likely to be long, some instrumental music on cassette may be an appropriate way of providing this.

-ooOoo-

HOW TO PRAY WITH PARTICIPANTS
FOR THE RELEASE OF THE HOLY SPIRIT

GENERAL ARRANGEMENT

In a parish or other large group seminar, one of the common ways of praying for the release of the Holy Spirit is as follows.

As soon as the Mass is over, the copies of the Prayer for New Life in the Holy Spirit are distributed and the team leader gives the introduction.

The celebrant or the team leader then reads out the prayer *just to familiarise participants with it.*

The group leaders then take up positions - in twos - around the room, grouping three chairs together so that the participants can sit with them while praying.

The celebrant or team leader invites those wishing to pray for new life in the Holy Spirit to go and pray with any 'pair' of group leaders. They can either use the prayer that has been distributed, or pray in their own words: whatever they feel most comfortable with. (Most participants like to have a written prayer that they feel covers what they want to say, and helps them to say it; a few prefer to pray spontaneously.)

K8

Participants coming to pray with the group leaders should be greeted, and invited to pray the prayer aloud with them, or to pray aloud in their own words, one of the leaders explaining that they are praying silently *in support of the participant* as he/she prays in this way (not sitting there merely as observers!), and that when the participant has finished they will pray briefly over them in the Spirit.

Once the participant has finished, the group leaders pray gently in tongues over the participant - audibly *but softly* - just for a couple of minutes.

After this time of prayer, and any word of prophecy that may have been given (see below), the leaders should simply thank the participant for the privilege of praying with them. They should also ask the participant, on returning to their place, to pray for those who have still to come forward to pray.

PROPHETIC WORDS FOR PARTICIPANTS

During this time of prayer, both the group leaders should be keenly alert to any word of prophecy that the Lord may wish to give them for the participant. If group leaders allow themselves to be fully open to the Lord in this way, it is quite common for *both* the leaders to be given a word for the participant, often confirmatory of the word given by the other. It should be explained to the participant that this word is a prophetic word from the Lord to them on this very special occasion.

YIELDING TO THE GIFT OF TONGUES

If a participant yields to the gift of tongues while they are being prayed with, one of the group leaders should confirm to the participant that he/she *is* praying in tongues, and the group leaders should pray in the Spirit with the participant for a couple of minutes. The participant should also be encouraged to continue to pray for a little while in tongues when he/she returns to their place.

RESTING IN THE HOLY SPIRIT

If during this prayer time a participant rests in the Holy Spirit, one of the group leaders should speak to them quietly, telling them that the Holy Spirit is now ministering to them directly in a very powerful way (very often in healing) and they will be left in quiet with Him while He does so.

It is important that people resting in the Holy Spirit do not force themselves to get up and return to their places before the Holy Spirit has finished what He wants to do! People are often tempted to 'struggle' to get up prematurely: group leaders need to help them to avoid that mistake by telling the participant to stay 'resting' in this way until he/she feels able to rise easily and return to their place.

It is *not* helpful for participants to have someone praying with them while they are resting in the Holy Spirit - unless they are distressed and need ministry. However, a group leader should generally keep an eye on them.

PROPHETIC WORDS FOR THE WHOLE GROUP

Sometimes the celebrant at Mass will mention during the thanksgiving after Communion that the Lord often gives various people words of encouragement for the group at this time, and invite the group to speak out anything that they feel the Lord is saying to the group in their hearts.

This can also happen after all the participants (so wishing) have been prayed with for the release of the Holy Spirit.

K8

-ooOoo-

PRAYING IN A SMALL GROUP SEMINAR FOR THE RELEASE OF THE HOLY SPIRIT

GENERAL ARRANGEMENT

An alternative way of praying for the release of the Holy Spirit which works very well if the whole group (team included) is small (say, around 25 people or fewer) is as follows:

Those wishing to pray for the release of the Holy Spirit are invited to stand in a circle, with the celebrant, speaker, team leader, group leaders and any other members of the team whom the leader thinks appropriate, all standing within the circle.

The celebrant or team leader first reads aloud the prayer for new life in the Holy Spirit, and then the whole group pray the prayer aloud together.

After the prayer, those within the circle pray in the Spirit (one-to-one) with the participants nearest them and, as they may be led, with other participants in the circle.

Once a participant has been prayed with, they should be invited to move out of the circle and to sit and pray quietly for those still being prayed with.

The remarks above on pages 110-111 regarding prophecy, tongues and resting in the Holy Spirit all apply, of course, in the same way to praying in this fashion.

-ooOoo-

HELPING PARTICIPANTS YIELD
TO THE GIFT OF TONGUES

The following sets out a very simple and effective way in which many participants can be helped to yield to the gift of tongues:

INVITATION
Ask the participants who wish to yield to the gift of tongues to gather in a large circle (not cramped together, but giving each other a little space), with the leader and team members who are praying with them grouped in the centre.
The invitation to join this session should also be extended to any participants who either think they *may* have prayed in tongues before (but are unsure), or who know they *have*, but have allowed the gift to fall into disuse - so that they can firmly re-establish their openness to this gift.

TEAM LEADER'S INTRODUCTION
The team leader should first remind participants of what they heard in the morning seminar concerning how to yield to the gift of tongues (as set out on page 16 of Part 2 of the **K8** Guide), namely, that once the leader has led the group in praying to the Holy Spirit, each participant then remains focused on the Lord - waiting silently in the quietness of their heart, in expectation - ready to speak out as and when they feel a physical prompting to do so by the Holy Spirit. When they sense that prompting, they should speak out, not

in their natural language, but surrendering their voice to the Holy Spirit, speaking whatever sounds He gives them. *It may help them if, in doing so, they try to imitate those praying in tongues with them: they won't manage to do so, but as soon as they try, they will* immediately *be given their own unique prayer in tongues.*

The team leader then explains how this prayer session will proceed, covering the following three points.

The team leader will first lead the group in a very short prayer (aloud) simply thanking the Holy Spirit for giving everyone the courage to come before Him in this way, and asking the Holy Spirit to help the participants to yield to Him, praying through them in the gift of tongues. (This prayer will take literally about 10 seconds.)

After that prayer, the team leader will begin immediately to pray in tongues, leading the team members in praying aloud together in the Spirit for the participants - for no more than half a minute.

The team members will then move, as they feel led by the Spirit, to pray in tongues with participants in the circle.

THE TEAM PRAYER

When praying in the centre of the circle, the team should pray 'strongly' (with enthusiasm!).

PRAYING ONE-TO-ONE WITH PARTICIPANTS

You will need to stand close to participants during this one-to-one prayer time, so that in addition to keeping an eye on their lip movements, you can *hear* them if they begin to pray aloud. Many participants start praying in tongues very faintly.

When praying with individual participants (again, 'strongly', *but not too loudly*) you should, of course, be praying in tongues in your normal way, and at your normal speed - not slowing it down or over-articulating so that the participant *can* imitate you!

If the participant does not begin to pray in tongues *within* about one minute *(one and a half minutes at the most!)* you should stop praying and ask them to share how they are feeling at this point. If they share that they are peaceful in their heart, focusing on the Lord, then tell them that you will continue to pray with them, but only for a further minute or so because you do not want them to become tired or to feel pressured.

You should then raise them up in tongues again, but only for a minute or two *(maximum!)*.

If the participant shares that they do not feel peaceful or do not seem able to stay quietly focused, you should tell them that it may not be all that helpful to continue if they are struggling, and that you will conclude by praying with them in thanksgiving for their courage in *asking* the Holy Spirit to help them yield to this gift. At the end of this prayer, reassure the participant on the lines indicated under the heading 'When a participant does not pray in tongues', **K8** below.

WHEN A PARTICIPANT BEGINS TO PRAY IN TONGUES
Whenever you hear a participant beginning to pray in tongues, you will readily recognise (in the Spirit) that they are doing so. *As soon as you do so, you should tell the*

participant that they are praying in tongues. It is very important encouragement for them to receive this early confirmation. (This same confirmation is especially important for those participants who think they may have prayed in tongues before, or have allowed the gift to fall into disuse.) The participant should then be encouraged to continue to pray out with you freely (and, if necessary, more audibly) in tongues, in thanksgiving.

After a minute or so (but no longer) of praying together in thanksgiving, the participant should be asked to continue to pray on their own for a little while in tongues for those participants to whom the team are still ministering.

WHEN A PARTICIPANT DOES NOT PRAY IN TONGUES

If a participant does not yield to the gift of tongues during this prayer time, you must reassure them that there are no 'failures' in this matter, that they are not being 'denied' this gift, and that they have already taken the vital step of *asking* the Holy Spirit to help them yield to Him in this special way.

Also encourage them to continue to be sensitive to the Holy Spirit's prompting to yield to tongues, explaining that this often happens while praying alone. In waiting on the Holy Spirit again, in the way they have learned today, (when they are fresh, and perhaps feeling freer praying alone), they should soon come into the gift of tongues. You should add, too, that there will be further opportunities, if they wish, for a member of the team to pray with them, following Seminars 9 and 10.

CONCLUDING REMARKS BY THE TEAM LEADER

When everyone has been prayed with, the team leader should conclude the session by asking for the whole group's attention to his closing remarks.

He/she should first briefly stress **again,** for the benefit of those who have not yet prayed in tongues, the points made under the heading 'When a participant does not pray in tongues' immediately above. These participants need 'double' reassurance that they haven't 'failed' where everyone else has 'succeeded' and encouragement to pray again soon on their own, or if they wish with a team member. (Refer them, finally, to the last paragraph on p. 18 of Part 2 of the Guide.)

He/She should then encourage those who have yielded to the gift of tongues by *briefly* mentioning the three points under the heading 'Once you have begun to pray in tongues' on pages 19/20 of Part 2 of the Guide, and recommend them to read through those pages *soon* for themselves.

PARTICIPANTS PRAYING FOR THE TEAM

If time (and energy!) permit after the leader's concluding remarks, it is a great blessing for the team (as well as a marvellous encouragement to the participants) if the leader now invites the participants to pray in a circle, extending their hands over the team gathered in the centre. The **K8** leader should explain that everyone (team included) will be praying aloud: those who can, praying in tongues, with the remainder praying in their own language.

This last prayer time of the day is often marked by the Lord speaking in prophecy - many speaking a prophetic word for the first time.

SECTION K/9

NOTES FOR SEMINAR 9

"ONLY HAVE FAITH"

PROGRAMME

30 min . . . . Welcome by the team leader
Prayer with an opportunity for
brief witness by participants
45 min . . . . Introduction of the speaker
Talk
35 min . . . . Small group discussion session
10 min . . . . Prayer
Notices

SPEAKER

PRAYER OF PROCLAMATION
Prayer of proclamation (recommended under the outline heading 'Develop an attitude of trust') - will be new to many participants. They should be encouraged to make it a 'standard' part of their prayer - a most powerful way in which the Lord builds us up in trusting Him in everything. The psalms, of course, provide one of the best ways of developing this form of prayer.

TURN 'MORNING OFFERING' INTO CONTINUAL OFFERING

St. Paul's exhortation to pray constantly needs to be emphasised and translated into practical terms. The tradition of praying the morning offering, recalled and raised up throughout our day, becomes the perfect application of what St.Paul has in mind.

TEAM LEADER

As part of your opening welcome, announce that any participant who missed Seminar 8 and who wishes to be prayed with for the release of the Holy Spirit should let their group leader know, and arrangements will be made for them to be prayed with at the end of the evening. Similarly, the team will be happy to pray at the end of the evening with anyone who wishes to yield to the gift of tongues.

This seminar opens with a prayer time devoted to thanksgiving. After the prayer, there is an excellent opportunity for participants to give just the briefest witness to what the Lord has been doing in their lives in these seminars.

If there are any participants whom you or a group leader knows might be happy (or could be easily persuaded!) to share in this way, ask them (ideally the day before the seminar) to say just a few words of witness during this opening prayer time.

The team leader (or, if appropriate, the speaker for the evening) should also issue a general invitation to the group at the end of the prayer time, inviting anyone who wishes to

K9

come forward to witness briefly as part of the group's thanksgiving.

Participants should be encouraged to use the microphone for their sharing.

There are three important matters to raise in the closing notices:

- Draw the participants' attention to the Section of their Guide entitled 'Prayers' which some may find helpful in response to the teaching at Seminar 9.
- Also draw their attention to the 'What Next?' form being distributed (see Admin Checklist on page 121). Encourage everybody to give it some thought and - if they do have any proposals for new parish group activities in which they would like to participate - to hand in their completed forms at Seminar 10.
- Encourage participants to read the article in their Guide entitled 'Where Do I Go from Here?'

In addition you may want to announce a retiring collection (see Admin Checklist on page 121).

GROUP LEADERS

Open the discussion time by asking each member of your group to share, if they wish, how the weekend seminars went for them, generally how they now feel about them (particularly Seminar 8), and any changes they have already begun to experience.

In responding to what they share, remember to draw on what

is said in the 'Afterword on Seminar 8' contained in Part 2 of the Guide. Take special care to reassure and encourage anyone who feels 'flat' or despondent, if necessary privately after the seminar.

Try to manage your time to allow at least *some* sharing by the participants on the Seminar 9 talk.

Depending on the turnout at this seminar, it may be appropriate to encourage everyone present to make sure they don't miss the last seminar, and to contact any missing members of your group to encourage them likewise.

BOOKSTALL

It may be appropriate to draw attention to some of the (new) titles available on the bookstall, particularly those relating to the gifts of the Holy Spirit.

Get in touch with the Good News Magazine office and also the publishers of Bible Alive each of whom will be happy to send you some *free* copies of their publication (possibly the latest) if they know that it is going to be specially promoted at Seminar 10.

ADMIN CHECKLIST

K9

Prepare forms for distribution at the end of this seminar inviting participants to put forward any suggestions they may have for new parish group activities *in which they would like to participate* once the seminars have ended. (An example - entitled 'What Next?' - is given on page 123.)

If your finances have not worked out as accurately as

anticipated, you may wish to announce in the closing notices that you are taking up a retiring collection at this seminar, and after Seminar 10, to try and cover the shortfall. (It is always helpful to tell the group how much the shortfall is.) Some gifts may now need to be bought for presentation at the end of Seminar 10. [See Team Leader's notes for Seminar 10.]

Prepare a leaflet giving the details of the follow-up programme and also listing times/venues of local prayer meetings, times/venues for adoration of the Blessed Sacrament etc. for distribution at the end of Seminar 10.

'WHAT NEXT?'

If, following these seminars, you would like to join with other participants in establishing a new group activity in the parish (e.g. a charismatic prayer group; evangelisation cell group; adoration of the Blessed Sacrament; daytime rosary group, etc.) please give details of your suggestion(s) below and return this form to the team leader at Seminar 10.
(If you need extra space, please use the back of the form.)

NAME (Block capitals please)

ACTIVITY

FREQUENCY/TIME (e.g.weekly/8 p.m Tuesdays)

HELP I CAN OFFER (e.g.training/teaching; transport/venue)

OTHER COMMENTS   **K9**

Names of any others in your group also interested in supporting this activity   (Please use block capitals)

SECTION K/10

NOTES for SEMINAR 10

"A NEW CREATION"

PROGRAMME

The programme for this seminar will be the same as for Seminar 3 (see page 84).

SPEAKER

COMPREHENSIVE OUTLINE

The outline for this talk is deliberately wide ranging with a view to enabling participants to take their bearings and give them some further clear guidelines as to the way forward. It is worth trying to cover the outline in your talk (maintaining a reasonably fast pace to do so), even though you will not be able to deal with subjects in great depth.

KNOWING WHO WE ARE

The opening emphasis on knowing who we are (our new identity) is of major significance. Unless participants really appreciate who they are- now that they have invited Jesus into the very centre of their lives - and their basic call to holiness, they will not have the understanding and vision required to sustain their efforts in prayer, studying and praying scripture, service etc. - all the things in which we are encouraging them now to persevere.

'ME - HOLY?!'

Holiness is at the heart of our call to discipleship, and many have a very warped idea of what holiness is all about. So often it is considered to be an unattainable ideal, something which we personally can never attain, indeed never intended to attain: it is for the odd 'saint', like Mother Teresa of Calcutta - not for the man in the street.

This is a fundamental misunderstanding that carries the most serious consequences. Unless we take Jesus at His word, and accept that *in Him* we are realistically called to holiness, we are unlikely to learn how to trust and live in the power of the Holy Spirit. As a result, we will revert to trying to live out the gospel in our own strength.

SIN IS ABNORMAL

The assertion that sin is abnormal is likely to make more than a few participants really sit up! Which only illustrates how seriously we can fail to enjoy the fruit of Jesus' victory on the cross. How easily we are convinced not only that we are miserable sinners, but that we're going to stay that way, *with little chance of any radical improvement!*

K10

This is to deny ourselves the very freedom that Jesus has won for us. Scripture abounds with the proclamation that sin no longer has any place in the life of a Christian (see in particular Romans 6 and the First letter of St.John). We will fall, of course, **but it should no longer be the norm.** The point is reinforced by the encouragement given by

125

Peter, Paul, John and James to actively put aside our old ways -something we can realistically expect to be able to do because we now have *His* power to do it!

PRAYING SCRIPTURE

The Participant's Guide encourages all participants to subscribe to 'Bible Alive'. There will probably be copies available either to purchase, or inspect, on the bookstall. Please mention this in your talk.

SERVICE OF OTHERS AND EVANGELISATION

The emphasis in relation to service is that we must do the Father's will. It is right to draw participants' attention to the fact that there are all sorts of service to be done within the community. What matters, however, for the individual is to discern what the *Father* wants them to do, how *He* wants them to serve. We have to listen first, and be led. We're no longer doing things *for* Him, but *with* Him.

The call of each one of us to witness to those around us is, of course, central to our calling as Christians, and is something we will begin to fulfil with greater impact as we move more freely in the power of the Holy Spirit.

PRAYER GROUPS

In touching on the subject of community, it is important to emphasise that the local prayer group(s) offer an important opportunity to grow in the Spirit with the support of others, and to help others in their turn to do so.

TEAM LEADER

At the end of this seminar:

- Thank the team, particularly members from outside your group or parish and anyone else who deserves special mention e.g. the music ministry (to whom you may wish to present a gift).
- Remind participants of the dates for the follow-up sessions and encourage everyone to make a special effort to come along to them.
- Call participants' attention again to the article in their Guide entitled: 'Where Do I Go from Here?' as well as to the leaflet being distributed setting out details of the follow-up programme and of the times/venues of local prayer meetings, times/venues for adoration of the Blessed Sacrament etc.

GROUP LEADERS

If anything should be re-emphasised in the discussion session, it is:

- The paramount importance of establishing and **K10** persevering with a daily time of prayer, and the need to read and pray scripture on a daily basis. Give your group every encouragement in this respect, urge them to continue with their prayer journal, and recommend them to subscribe to a scripture reading guide (preferably 'Bible Alive').

- The need to link up, if at all possible, with one of the local prayer groups which will provide ongoing support and the opportunity to grow in openness to the Holy Spirit.
- Encourage any members of your group who wish to participate in new parish group activities to complete their 'What Next?' form as early as possible (ideally at the end of this seminar) and return it to the team leader. You should have some spare copies of the form.

ADMIN CHECKLIST

Leaflets are to be available for distribution at the close of this seminar giving details of the follow-up programme and times/venues of local prayer meetings etc.

Spare copies of the 'What Next?' form need to be available.

Gifts may need to be available for presentation by the team leader at the close of this seminar.

-ooOoo-

SECTION L

FOLLOW-UP
TO THE SEMINARS

THE NEED FOR COMMUNITY

The need for our parishes to develop as real communities of close Christian fellowship is both obvious and urgent. Those who have now embarked on a new life, lived in the power of the Holy Spirit, should be helped to appreciate that they have their role to play in building up the Christian community.

It is right in this context to encourage participants to become part of the fellowship and community that may be found in their local/parish prayer group. They will undoubtedly need the support and encouragement of like-minded Christians, not least in these early days of growing in Christian maturity.

At the same time, however, no-one should lose sight of the fact that the prayer group's natural outreach is in the parish(es) represented by its members. Furthermore, all of us should be continually encouraged by the knowledge that the Holy Spirit is renewing the whole church, which means that the ultimate destiny of our local prayer group is to disappear as something indistinguishable from the parish as a whole, which has become a community of believers enlivened by the Holy Spirit.

L

BUILDING ON THE SEMINARS

The seminars are, of course, only a beginning. It is outside the scope of this Handbook, however, to consider the steps that a group or parish might take in the longer term to allow the Lord to build on the foundations He has now laid.

There are, however, some very practical contributions which the team can make immediately to the continued growth of the participants, namely, the holding of a re-union for the whole group, and of workshops on the gifts of the Holy Spirit (in particular on tongues and prophecy) - all of which should ideally take place within two/three months of Seminar 10.

One of the best courses published to date intended principally as a follow up to Life in the Spirit seminars is that written by Fr.Bob Faricy S.J. and Sister Lucy Rooney, S.N.D. entitled 'Lord Jesus, Teach Me to Pray' - published by ICCRO. This is a seven week course in which participants are helped to pray through a daily scripture programme (with excellent guidance notes), meeting each week to pray and share together in small groups. At each meeting there is a short talk (10/15 minutes) - set out in full in the course material - and all the talks can be easily presented by two or three members of the group itself, without the need to invite 'outside' speakers. Serious consideration should be given to running this course as part of any follow-up programme.

SEMINARS RE-UNION

A programme for a re-union supper is set out on pages 132-133.

WORKSHOP ON THE GIFT OF TONGUES

A programme for a workshop on the gift of tongues is set out on pages 135-137.

WORKSHOP ON THE GIFT OF PROPHECY

A programme for a workshop on the gift of prophecy, together with detailed guidance on running the workshop, and an article on which the talk can be based, are contained at the end of this section, on pages 138-151.

-ooOoo-

L

THE SEMINARS RE-UNION

TIMING

Whatever may be the timing generally of the follow-up programme, the re-union is best held about three weeks after Seminar 10. There is the danger that if it is left longer than this, some participants will start to lose interest and contact.

PROGRAMME

The programme for a re-union supper might run as follows:

19.15	**Team briefing and prayer time**
19.45	**Welcome participants**
19.45 - 20.10	**Laying out buffet food**
20.10 - 20.15	**Team leader's welcome with opening prayer**
20.15 - 20.20	**Team leader's explanation of the format for the evening**
20.20 - 21.10	**Buffet supper**

Before the supper begins the team leader should encourage participants to circulate periodically - introducing themselves to/and sharing with participants outside their original group. (Group leaders should give similar encouragement (and example) during the supper itself.)

21.10 - 21.45	**Small group sharing**

Before the small group sharing, the team leader should explain that this group sharing should cover what has been going on in your spiritual life since the end of the seminars, in particular addressing the following questions:

What did you decide to *do* following the end of the seminars?' (This is referring to the article at the end of the Guide: 'Where Do I Go from Here?')
Have you been able to follow that through?'
How has your prayer life been going generally?'
Have you continued to pray scripture regularly?'
Are you still keeping your prayer journal?'
Have you formed (or started to attend) a prayer meeting?'
How is that working out for you?'

21.45 - 21.55   **Team leader's synopsis of feedback from the 'What Next?' forms**

As a preliminary point, it is not necessarily a good idea to have open, 'on-the-spot' feedback by group leaders to the team leader and the rest of the participants at the end of the small group sharing. (A *poor* report back from a particular group - along the lines of: 'Nobody's really doing much in our group: not even praying regularly' - would be very embarrassing and unhelpful for the group in question.) The team leader needs to take a careful sounding from the group leaders before inviting 'open' feedback from this time of sharing. L

The team leader can, however, very usefully present here a brief synopsis of whatever feedback he/she has received in the 'What Next?' forms, and take the opportunity to put participants in touch with those who are interested in facilitating the same things e.g. forming a prayer group; starting an evangelisation cell; organising a rota for adoration of the Blessed Sacrament etc.

21.55   **Closing prayer**
                   Notices
                   (in particular concerning
                   the follow-up programme.)

ADMIN CHECKLIST

Participants should be contacted by their group leaders shortly before the re-union is due to take place to encourage them to come along.

It will be helpful to have a small card/leaflet for each of the participants when they move into their small group sharing, setting out the questions they should address.

The team leader might wish to circulate an information sheet relating to proposed new group activities, with contact names/telephone numbers etc.

-ooOoo-

WORKSHOP
on
THE GIFT OF TONGUES

INTRODUCTION

It is vital to give some continued help to participants to become more and more open to the giftedness of the Holy Spirit working within them. Notwithstanding the fact that many of the participants will have already yielded to the gift of tongues, it is certain that some will not, and a number will be struggling to persevere with the use of this gift. The purpose of the workshop, therefore, is twofold:

- to help anyone who has not yet yielded
  to this gift, to do so
- to encourage all those who have yielded to it,
  to persevere in its use.

In addition, the workshop will help many participants to become open (at the next workshop) to the gift of prophecy.

It should be explained that those participants who have yielded, and who *are* persevering, should attend the workshop to give thanks and to pray for their fellow participants.

L

PROGRAMME

The programme for the evening might run as follows:

20 min . . . . Welcome by the team leader
Prayer
30 min . . . . Introduction of the workshop
Introduction of the speaker
Talk on the gift of tongues
20 min . . . . Prayer with all those who wish to be prayed
with to yield to, or be encouraged in using,
the gift of tongues.
10 min . . . . Exhortation to persevere in this gift on the
lines referred to in the paragraph headed
'Concluding remarks by the team leader'
at the end of the Notes for Seminar 8
(see page 117).
10 min . . . . Closing prayer.

SPEAKER

Bearing in mind that almost everyone attending this
workshop will have heard the original talk on the gift of
tongues given in part 2 of Seminar 6, this talk should be no
more than a resume of the main points of the original talk,
covering the scriptural background to the gift, its purposes,
and how to yield to tongues.

TEAM LEADER

INTRODUCTION OF THE WORKSHOP

Just before their introduction of the speaker, the team leader should explain that a 'workshop' (properly so called) embraces three things: prayer, teaching, and opening to the Holy Spirit in prayer, inviting Him to *act!*

This opening remark helps participants to realise that they have not come just to hear a talk, but to pray with expectation that the Holy Spirit will help them this evening to yield to the gift of tongues.

TEAM

The guidance notes under the heading: 'Helping participants yield to the Gift of Tongues' for Seminar 8 (see pages 113-117) recommends how the team leader and other team members may pray with participants at this workshop.

-ooOoo-

L

WORKSHOP
on
THE GIFT OF PROPHECY

PROGRAMME

15 min . . . .Welcome by team leader
Prayer
40 min . . . . Introduction of the workshop*
Introduction of the speaker
Talk on the gift of prophecy
10/15 . . . .Opening to prophecy in small groups
30 min . . . .*Plenary session - sharing with the
whole group some of the prophecies
received in the small groups - with
prayer response led by the speaker
5 min . . . .Closing remarks and prayer

* N.B. The 'plenary session' of the programme should **not** be mentioned in the introduction of the workshop (see further below). It is enough to say in the introduction that, following the talk, there will be a time of prayer asking the Holy Spirit to open our hearts to the gift of prophecy.

TEAM LEADER AND SPEAKER

HOW TO HELP PARTICIPANTS YIELD TO THE
GIFT OF PROPHECY
Guidance on helping participants yield to the gift of prophecy is given on page 140-143.

INTRODUCTION OF THE WORKSHOP
As in the case of the workshop on tongues, just prior to their introduction of the speaker, the team leader should remind participants that a 'workshop' comprises three things: prayer, teaching and opening in prayer to the Holy Spirit inviting Him to *act!*
This opening remark helps participants to realise that they have not come just to hear a talk, but to pray with expectation that the Holy Spirit will help them this evening to yield to the gift of prophecy.

THE TALK
The talk can be based on the article on the gift of prophecy at the end of this section - commencing on page 144.
After the talk, the session should move immediately into a time of prayer. A general 'question time' is not appropriate at this stage. It will risk losing the participants' focus on what the speaker has emphasised, and also the general momentum of the workshop.

L

-ooOoo-

HELPING PARTICIPANTS YIELD
TO THE GIFT OF PROPHECY

The following sets out a very simple and effective way in which many participants can be helped to yield to the gift of prophecy. The notes refer throughout to 'the speaker' assuming (as will usually be the case) that he/she will lead the prayer session.

EXPLAINING THE PRAYER SESSION

The speaker should explain how this prayer session will proceed, covering the following six points:

- Everyone will divide to form groups of four or five - one group leader to three or four participants. (It is not necessary for participants to be with the same group leader they had for the seminars.)
- The group leaders will lead each group in asking the Holy Spirit to help them to yield to Him in the gift of prophecy, and then in praying together in tongues (audibly but softly) for about one minute - *but not longer!* (Alternatively, the speaker may wish to lead the whole group in this brief opening prayer.)
- Everyone then listens in the quietness of their heart, waiting in silence on the Holy Spirit, and speaking out quietly (but audibly!) to the group as and when they receive a word of prophecy.
- When someone in the group has spoken a word of prophecy, the rest should each respond to it quietly

(and preferably audibly) in prayer, as they may feel led, as mentioned in the talk. The group then continues to wait in silence on the Holy Spirit for further words of prophecy.

- If someone receives a word in tongues, or a visual prophecy that requires interpretation, then the group should ask the Holy Spirit for the interpretation - again as mentioned in the talk.
- The speaker will bring this time of prayer to a close after approximately 10 minutes.

The speaker should not at this stage mention the 'plenary' session, which will follow the small groups' prayer time. To do so could easily deter some participants from opening themselves to receive a word of prophecy at this time.

SEATING ARRANGEMENTS

The speaker should then invite all the participants to move quietly into groups. (The speaker should not join one of the small groups. This can often inhibit a small group from opening up.)

If numbers do not work out neatly, some groups may need to be six. Note, however, that groups of less than four may feel 'pressured' and will not work so well.

The participants in each group should sit close together so that they can share their prophecy and pray together without too much distraction for adjacent groups.

The groups themselves should be reasonably spread out to avoid distracting each other.

L

MONITORING AND CLOSING THE SMALL GROUP PRAYER SESSION

The speaker should remain in the room with everyone during the small group session, sitting apart from the groups and just raising everyone up in prayer.

Some groups do take time to open up, and the speaker may find that at the ten-minute mark some groups have only recently 'warmed up' and still seem to be sharing prophecy. If that is the case, allow a few more minutes before closing the small group session at a point when the groups are silent. Close down the small group session in any event after fifteen minutes have elapsed, otherwise participants in some groups may start to feel uncomfortable.

THE 'PLENARY' SESSION

When the speaker has called the small group prayer session to a close, they should ask the groups to stay together, but to move closer to the other groups, for the next part of the workshop.

The speaker then explains that the prophecy received in the small groups would benefit everyone present - indeed in normal circumstances it *would* have been spoken for everyone to hear.

In view of this, the speaker then invites anyone who is willing to do so, to share aloud with the whole group the prophecy they received during the small group session. For this purpose a 'roving' microphone is very helpful; otherwise the speaker should make sure everyone has heard, if necessary repeating the prophecy aloud.

After each prophecy shared, the speaker leads the group in

a very short prayer of response to it.
If a group shares a visual prophecy that required interpretation, they should of course also share the interpretation they were given. If the group did not receive an interpretation, then the speaker should lead the whole group in prayer for interpretation.
In the normal course of this session quite a number of prophecies will confirm prophecies given in other groups - which is very upbuilding for all concerned.

CLOSING THE 'PLENARY' SESSION

The speaker should end the workshop by thanking everyone for taking part, and for praying together and contributing in the way they have.

It is important that the speaker makes it clear that there are no 'failures' in this workshop, emphasising that although a word is not given to everybody in the course of a prayer time such as this, *the prophecy received is a result of the whole group's prayer.* Furthermore, those who were not personally given a word for the group on this particular occasion *took the vital step of making themselves available to the Holy Spirit in this gift of prophecy.* Continued openness to this gift on everyone's part is crucial to the freedom of the Holy Spirit in speaking God's word to His people.

Finally, the speaker leads the group in a short prayer of thanksgiving to the Holy Spirit for all the love and encouragement experienced by the group during the prayer session, through His prophetic word spoken through His people.

THE GIFT OF PROPHECY

'Make love your aim;
then be eager for the gifts of the Spirit,
above all for prophecy.'

1 Cor.14-1 (REB)

WHAT IS PROPHECY?

Prior to the seminars, many participants may have felt God speaking to them occasionally during their lives, but these will tend to have been isolated, private experiences. Prophecy as experienced during the seminars, however, will have been something totally new for most of those taking part.

It comes as a surprise to find that, just as we can *know* God just as He is *in* us and *with* us, so He also *speaks* to us. The secular, everyday understanding of the word 'prophecy' falls far short of its fullest meaning as a charismatic gift. Isaiah 6:8-9 tells us what prophecy means: a prophet is a spokesman/woman for God, and prophecy is *speaking God's word to His people.*

GIFT TO WHICH ALL SHOULD BE OPEN

It is important for the purposes of this article to distinguish between a gift to which all should be open, and a gift through which some are called to minister in a special way to the community. Where a person's principal service to the body

144

of Christ is currently in the exercise of a particular gift, then that person is discerned by the community as having a *ministry* relating to that gift. Obvious examples would be the prophetic ministry of Clifford Hill, or the healing ministry of Francis MacNutt. However, while only a *few* may be called to prophetic *ministry*, **all** Christians are called to be open to the Holy Spirit to receive God's word and proclaim it to His people.

In 1 Cor.14, Paul encourages **everyone** to be open to the action of the Holy Spirit within them, enabling them to speak in prophecy.

We may need to remind ourselves that we have received the Holy Spirit in all His fullness, in all *His* giftedness, and each of us is called to be His instrument, to be used just as He pleases. The gift of prophecy - like all the charisms of the Holy Spirit - is one of the 'tools for the job' designed to meet the needs of God's people in completing the work on earth begun by Jesus.

PROPHECY BRINGS LIFE

Isaiah 55:10-11 illustrates the essential nature of prophecy. The word of the Lord in prophecy is alive and active: *it brings life!*

More specifically, the prophetic word may:
- encourage [see Haggai 2:3-5]
- inspire - building up our relationship with the Lord
- convict [see 1 Cor.14:24-25]
- direct
- foretell

L

'HOW DO I RECEIVE PROPHECY?'

The various ways in which we receive prophecy are as follows:

1) Actual words of a message

Actual words come into your mind, forming a message. It is not uncommon for a series of messages to be received in this way (usually by various members of the group) which together make up what is known as a 'teaching prophecy'.

2) A few 'opening' words

Similarly, actual words come into your mind, but they seem to be the opening words of a message. When you begin to speak the words out, the rest of the message is given to you.

3) The general sense of a message

In this instance you receive no words, but just a general sense of a message (on a specific theme), which the Lord wants to give. As you begin to speak out, the actual words are given to you.

4) Prophecy in tongues

Sometimes a prophetic message is given in tongues. In such a case the group must pray for an interpretation to be given (The interpretation will normally be given to someone other than the person who has spoken the prophecy in tongues.)

5) Visual prophecy

You can also receive prophecy in the form of a picture coming into your mind. This is a very common form of prophecy When you receive a prophecy in this way, simply describe the picture you have been given. Usually the picture speaks for itself. If it does not, the group must pray for an interpretation - just as in the case of a prophecy in tongues A good example of visual prophecy can be found in Jeremiah

1:11-14 in which God gives Jeremiah pictures in his mind, and then gives him their interpretation.

6) Prophecy from scripture

Prophecy is also given in the form of a passage from scripture, with either the verse(s) coming into your mind, or the passage being given to you on reading the bible (often on opening the bible at random).

7) Prophecy in action

This is a comparatively rare form of prophecy, in which a person is prompted by the Holy Spirit to act out a prophetic message - as illustrated, for example, in the incident of the prophecy given to Paul through the prophet Agabus as recorded in Acts 21:10-11.

TWO VITAL CHARACTERISTICS OF ALL PROPHECIES

All prophecies have two vital characteristics in common:

- The word or picture is recognised as not your own - not coming from yourself.
- It is accompanied by a growing sense of being urged to speak it out.

[Prophetic action would also share these two characteristics, with the urging referred to being to act it out.]

TEST YOUR WORD OR PICTURE

It is important that when you *first* receive what may be a prophetic word or picture, you yourself test it. That is **not** to say that you are the judge as to whether or not it is truly prophetic: that is the responsibility of those to whom it is spoken (see 'Discerning Prophecy' below). Your 'initial' testing means in practice the following:

L

147

When a word or a picture comes into your mind, you 'hold' it to see if it has the two vital characteristics mentioned above - asking the question: 'Is this just me?', and seeing whether you sense an urging to speak it out.

The Holy Spirit helps us to recognise fairly easily when something is not 'just me', but from Him. In addition, the same words or picture remain in our mind, or return to our mind, with an insistent urging to speak them out, which again we recognise as a prompting by the Holy Spirit. So it is important not to wrestle too much with the question: 'Is this just me?' If it *seems* not to be you, and there is a growing urge to speak it out, then do so. If in doubt, it is important to *give the benefit of the doubt to the Holy Spirit!*

You must not pass judgement on the word or picture you are given. It does not matter, for example, if the content of a picture seems rather unusual - it is not your responsibility to offer the interpretation of it (unless, of course, the Holy Spirit also gives you the interpretation) - or if a word strikes you as strange or possibly trivial. It may be extremely important to those for whom it is intended.

Particular care needs to be taken in this personal 'testing' in the case of prophecy from scripture. All scripture is inspired, but whether a passage is being given in *prophecy* is another matter. When the Lord is speaking to a group in prophecy, you need to guard against just speaking out some 'favourite' verses of your own accord, rather than speaking from scripture under the prompting of the Holy Spirit.

SPEAKING OUT YOUR WORD OR PICTURE

As with all the gifts of the Holy Spirit, their use is totally under our control. It is important, therefore, to judge what is the right time and place to speak out a prophecy. In particular, time must be given for people to respond to a prophecy, so (with the exception of something like a teaching prophecy) it is important for a prophecy not to be spoken out immediately after another, without allowing for some response time in between.

Be absolutely faithful to actual words or pictures you are given - don't change them in any way or try to 'improve' on them.

Speak out your prophecy in your normal voice: the Lord's word doesn't need enhancing or re-enforcing by being spoken dramatically.

In the case of a prophecy of which you initially only receive the general sense - item 3) under 'How do I receive prophecy?' - speak simply in a way that comes naturally to you: make no attempt to adopt a style or vocabulary you think may be more impressive or congenial to your listeners.

RESPONDING TO PROPHECY AND CONFIRMING PROPHECY

If someone speaks a word (or gives a picture) which encourages you or inspires you and really strikes you as the Lord's word - respond in prayer! If you can share your prayer response aloud with the group, so much the better.

If you received the same word (which often happens) or words very similar, or the same picture, you should immediately confirm what has been spoken out by saying: 'I confirm that. I was given the words............. and say the words you were given before the other person spoke out.

L

This confirmation of prophecy is very important both for the person who first spoke the prophecy, and for the group receiving it.

It is also good to privately affirm a person who has given a prophetic word when you have the opportunity. (An example might be: 'Thank you for that word.. it spoke deeply to my needs this evening' or whatever may be an appropriate affirmation.)

DISCERNING PROPHECY

It is the *community* that discerns prophecy - whether it is indeed the Lord's word to His people.

This discernment is most often an immediate discernment on the part of the group to whom the word is given. Where a word/picture is given 'in the Spirit', it strikes a note with a special kind of reverberation within us. The Holy Spirit dwelling in each of us, the body, quickens our response 'deep down' to the word given by Him through an individual in the group.

Another aspect of discernment that is closely linked to the last is that, to the *listener*, a word spoken in prophecy usually has a certain zesty, arresting quality about it, which marks it as being of the Spirit.

Another important test in the discernment of prophecy is: 'Does this word bear fruit?' Again, this fruit is often immediately evident in the prayer response of the group members. In many cases there will also be other fruit that becomes apparent in the longer term.

It is obvious, too, that in the discernment process any word must be disregarded if it conflicts in any way with scripture or the truths of Christianity as taught by the Church.

SUBMISSION TO THE GROUP'S DISCERNMENT

It is vital that those who find that the Holy Spirit is using them in the gift of prophecy are fully open to any correction or guidance that the leadership of the group may give them. Without this submission, they cannot grow in the use of this gift in the service of the group, and everyone suffers as a consequence.

REMAIN OPEN TO THE GIFT OF PROPHECY

There is a common temptation to assume that 'others' in a group will be speaking in prophecy and to allow them to 'get on with it!'   It is important to recognise and resist this temptation.

We are *all* called to be channels of God's loving service to others, and we need to live and move in the Spirit at all times. To do this, we need to be constant in 'stirring up' the gift of the Holy Spirit within ourselves personally, so as to remain as open to the Holy Spirit in speaking His prophetic word as we are to the manifestation in ourselves of all His other gifts.

-ooOoo-

L

RECOMMENDED READING
FOR TEAM AND GROUP LEADERS

Over the last thirty years there has been a vast amount of excellent spiritual writing on many aspects of renewal. An extensive list of recommended reading appears at the end of Part 2 of the Participant's Guide. The following books, however, are recommended as being among the best in their field and of particular help to team and group leaders - both in preparation for the seminars, and in relation to advice, encouragement and ministry to participants. (Titles listed in italics are out of print at the time of going to press, but they are sufficiently important to include in the hope that copies may be borrowed or acquired second-hand.)

Renewal
A New Pentecost?,Cardinal Suenens,DLT
Your God?,Cardinal Suenens,DLT
One Lord,One Spirit,One Body,Fr.Peter Hocken,Ave Maria
Disciple,Juan Carlos Ortiz,*Lakeland*
Cry of the Human Heart,Juan Carlos Ortiz,Lakeland

Autobiography
Prison to Praise,Merlin Carothers,*Hodder*
The Cross and the Switchblade,David Wilkerson,*Marshall*
Pickering
Beyond the Cross and the Switchblade,David Wilkerson,
Marshall Pickering
Chasing the Dragon,Jackie Pullinger,*Hodder*
Miracles do Happen,Sr.Briege McKenna O.S.C. *Pan Books*

When the Spirit Comes,Colin Urquhart,Hodder
Faith for the Future,Colin Urquhart,Hodder
His God, My God,Caroline Urquhart,Hodder

Priests' Testimonies
Anointed with The Spirit,Intr.by Bishop Langton D. Fox,
                            Mayhew-McCrimmon
The Lord is My Shepherd,Intr. by Fr. George Kosicki,C.S.B.
                                    Servant
Renewed by the Spirit, Fr. Bob de Grandis, *available from*
                            Goodnews Books Books
Our Lady
Life in the Spirit and Mary,Fr.C.O.Donnell,O.Carm., *Michael*
                                    Glazier
Prayer
Come, Holy Spirit, Dom Benedict Heron,OSB, *New Life*
Pray with The Heart,Fr.Slavko Barbaric,O.F.M.,*Franc Univ*
Lord Jesus, Teach Me to Pray,Fr.R.Faricy,S.J. & Sr.
                    L.Rooney, S.N.D.,*ICCRO*
Seeking Jesus in Contemplation and Discernment,
                    Fr.R.Faricy,S.J., Collins
Miracle Hour ,Linda Schubert,*Available from Goodnews Books*
Too Busy Not to Pray,Bill Hybels,*Alpha*

Praying Scripture
Reading Scripture as the Word of God,George Martin,
                                    Servant
How to Pray the Rosary,Sr.M.Francis,*McCrimmon P.C.C.*
The Bible's Ways of Prayer,Fr.Wilfrid Harrington,O.P.   **M**
                        Dominican Publications

Fasting
Fasting,Fr. Slavko Barbaric,O.F.M.,*Franciscan Univ. Press*

Forgiveness
To Forgive is Divine, Fr.Robert DeGrandis, S.S.J.,
Available from Goodnews Books

The Sacraments
This is My Body,Fr.Ian Petit,O.S.B.,*DLT*
Celebrate Mass With your Heart,Fr.Slavko Barbaric,O.F.M.,
Faith Publishing Milford, OH
Give Me Your Wounded Heart (Reconciliation),Fr.Slavko
Barbaric,O.F.M.,*Franciscan Univ. Press*
The Power in Penance,Fr.M.Scanlon,T.O.R.,Notre Dame
To Heal as Jesus Healed - Sacrament of Anointing of the
Sick,Barbara Shlemon,D. & M.Linn,S.J.,*Ave Maria Press*

Gifts of the Holy Spirit
Come Holy Spirit,David Pytches,*Hodder*
Baptised in the Spirit And Spiritual Gifts,Steve Clark,
Servant

Healing
Healing* ,Francis MacNutt,*Hodder*
The Prayer that Heals,Francis MacNutt,*Hodder*
Praying for Healing,Fr.Benedict Heron, O.S.B.,*New Life
Publishing*
*The Healing Power Of the Sacraments,Fr.J.McManus,
C.Ss.R.,Redemptorist Publications*
Healing through The Mass,Fr.Robert DeGrandis,S.S.J.,
Available from Goodnews Books
*This is the best all round introduction to praying for healing.

Inner Healing
Healing the Hidden Self,Barbara Shlemon,*Ave Maria Press*
Healing in the Spirit,Fr.J.McManus,C.Ss.R,*DLT*
Inner Healing,Fr.Michael Scanlon,T.O.R.,*Paulist Press*
Healing the Dying,Sr.Mary JaneLinn,C.S.J.,*Paulist Press*
Healing of Self Image,Betty Tapscott & DeGrandis S.S.J.,
Available from Goodnews Books

Deliverance
The Ministry of Deliverance in the Catholic Tradition,
Fr.J.McManus,C.Ss.R.,*NSC [Pamphlet]*
Deliverance from Evil Spirits,Francis MacNutt, Ave Maria
Deliverance from Evil Spirits,Fr.Michael Scanlon,T.O.R. &
R.J.Cirner, *Servant*
* This is the most comprehensive of the books listed on this subject. MacNutt's book entitled 'Healing' also has an excellent introduction to deliverance.

Spiritual Warfare
I Saw Satan Fall,Fr.Benedict Heron,O.S.B.,*New Life Publishing*
Spiritual Warfare,Fr. George Kosicki,C.S.B.,*Faith Publishing*
Spiritual Warfare,Derek Prince,*Derek Prince Ministries*
[Booklet]

Evangelising
Becoming a Contagious Christian,Bill Hybels,*Alpha*

Prayer Groups
Growing Christians In Small Groups*,John Mallison
Scripture Union
* This must be the most practical, comprehensive, well written guide to establishing and running prayer groups (of all kinds) ever published.

Further copies of this Handbook
and the Participant's Guides 1 & 2
are available from:

Goodnews Books & Audio

Tel: 01582 571011
Fax: 01582 571012

www.goodnewsbooks.net
orders@goodnewsbooks.net

Other New Life Publishing titles
also available from Goodnews Books:

Joy in Heaven,
Fr. Luke Bell, OSB
God is a Feast,
A New Look at St. John of the Cross
Fr. Pius Sammut
"I Saw Satan Fall", the Ways of Spiritual
Warfare
Dom Benedict Heron, OSB
Praying for Healing, the Challenge,
Dom Benedict Heron, OSB
Come, Holy Spirit, help us to pray
Dom Benedict Heron, OSB

Goodnews Books are distributors for
"I Am With You" by Fr. John Woolley

Catalogue of Christian Books
and music available

NOTES

NOTES

NOTES

NOTES

NOTES

NOTES